ISBN-13

E-book: 978-1-972177-30-3

Soft cover: 978-1-972177-31-0

Metadata Failures in Large Book Platforms

By

James Curran

This book is a nonfiction historical record compiled from publicly visible discussions, user reports, and catalog behavior observed on the Goodreads platform specifically during a defined period of time. It is not a legal document and does not make legal claims or allegations. Its purpose is to preserve a snapshot of how authors, readers, volunteers, and staff publicly described their experiences with metadata, attribution, and catalog management on a social cataloging site.

All examples included here were publicly accessible at the time of compilation. They are presented for documentary and educational purposes, to help authors understand how the Goodreads catalog system appeared to behave from the outside and what challenges users reported when interacting with it. The commentary in this book reflects my interpretation of patterns visible in the public record and should be understood as analysis, not accusation.

This work does not claim to represent the internal policies, intentions, or operations of Goodreads or its parent company. It does not assert wrongdoing, and it does not offer legal advice. It simply preserves a moment in time—one that may be useful to authors, publishers, researchers, and historians studying how public-facing catalog systems function and how user-reported issues manifest within them.

Because online platforms evolve quickly, the conditions described here may not reflect current or future behavior. This book should be read as a historical snapshot of publicly visible interactions on Goodreads during this period, not as a prediction or a statement about any company's present practices.

Contents

Digital cataloging platforms have become essential tools for authors, readers, and publishers. They influence how books are discovered, how authors are identified, and how literary records are organized. Yet the systems behind these platforms are often opaque, and the experiences of authors navigating them are rarely documented in a structured way.

This book was compiled to better understand how metadata behaves within the Goodreads catalog specifically, as seen through publicly visible interactions. Over time, I observed recurring questions and challenges raised by authors and librarians in Goodreads discussion threads—questions about attribution, identity, catalog stability, and the persistence of errors. These conversations offered a unique window into how the system appeared to function from the outside, based solely on what users, volunteers, and staff stated publicly.

The purpose of this work is not to judge or criticize Goodreads or its parent company, but to preserve a snapshot of these publicly visible interactions so that authors can better understand the environment in which their books are listed. Metadata is foundational to discoverability and author identity, and even small inconsistencies can influence how a writer's work is presented to the world. By compiling these incidents into a single historical record, this book aims to provide clarity, context, and a broader view of the patterns that emerged in public discussions during this period.

This is a document of observation, not accusation. It reflects what could be seen publicly at a particular moment in time and is offered as a resource for authors, researchers, and anyone interested in how a public-facing catalog system behaves from the user perspective. As platforms evolve, the issues described here may change as well. What follows is simply a record of what was visible, what was discussed, and what could be learned from the conversations that took place.

Context and Overview

This chapter documents a publicly visible discussion in the Goodreads Librarians Group in March 2026. In that exchange, an author who appeared to be rebranding and separating from a previous publisher asked that several titles be removed from their Goodreads author page. The discussion may offer insight into how Goodreads librarians interpret book-removal requests, how platform guidelines are communicated in public forums, and how authors might experience limitations when attempting to manage their catalog presence on the site.

This chapter preserves the discussion exactly as it appeared, without alteration, as part of the historical record.

Snapshot Transcript (Verbatim)

Goodreads Librarians Group discussion *Book & Author Page Issues > Book removal request 10 views Comments Showing 1–5 of 5 Date: March 9, 2026*

message 1: by [deleted user] (new) *Mar 09, 2026 08:01AM* "Hello, I am rebranding and cutting ties with my current publisher, so I would like to have all of Christmas Day the books on my profile removed. *Signs In The Rearview Mirror: Leaving a Toxic Relationship Behind, Out Of The Darkness, The Wedding, The Pieces We Break*. Thank you."

message 2: by Scott (new) *Mar 09, 2026 08:03AM* "No. We don't remove out of print books."

message 3: by Scott (new) *Mar 09, 2026 08:04AM* "These are all still available from Amazon anyway."

message 4: by [deleted user] (new) *14 hours, 2 min ago* "Christmas Day is NOT available. When can you remove the books?"

message 5: by Scott (new) *2 hours, 38 min ago* "Please refer again to msg. #2."

Analysis and Interpretation

- Authors may not be able to remove their own books from Goodreads. In this discussion, the author appears to rely on a librarian to make catalog adjustments when rebranding or changing publishing arrangements.

- Librarians may interpret guidelines as limiting book removal. In this instance, the librarian refers to a guideline about not removing out-of-print titles, which may reflect how the rule was understood in this particular conversation.

- Amazon availability may be used as a reference point. The librarian's response cites Amazon listing status when considering whether the books should remain in the catalog, suggesting that availability on Amazon might influence how some requests are evaluated.

- Author pages may not be directly editable by authors. Based on this exchange, Goodreads appears to maintain catalog entries independently of an author's current branding or publishing status.

- No alternative pathway is mentioned in this discussion. In this specific example, the author does not appear to receive a publicly stated method for updating their work.

Taken together, this incident may reflect a pattern visible in several public discussions from the same period: catalog entries on Goodreads can appear persistent, and authors may find that their ability to modify or remove older titles is limited. The reference to Amazon availability in this example may also suggest how some librarians interpret removal requests. This chapter documents one publicly visible instance of how these guidelines were communicated and how an author appeared to experience them during this interaction.

This chapter documents a publicly visible discussion in the Goodreads Librarians Group in March 2026. In that exchange, an author named Michael O'Rourke reported that his book appeared to have been attributed to the wrong author profile. A librarian adjusted the attribution and created a new author page for him to claim. Within a day, the correction seemed to revert, and the book was reassigned to the earlier, incorrect author profile.

This incident may illustrate how Goodreads' cataloging processes or automated ingestion features could potentially override manual librarian adjustments, resulting in repeated misattribution even after an author claims their page. The transcript is preserved exactly as it appeared.

Snapshot Transcript (Verbatim)

Goodreads Librarians Group discussion *Book & Author Page Issues > Book attributed to wrong author 4 views Comments Showing 1–4 of 4 Date: March 8, 2026*

message 1: by Michael (new) *Mar 08, 2026 10:43AM* "Hi there, My book is attributed to the wrong Michael O'Rourke.
https://www.goodreads.com/book/show/2.. (goodreads.com in Bing).
Could you please move it to this Michael O'Rourke?
https://www.goodreads.com/user/show/1.. (goodreads.com in Bing).
Thank you so much for your help! Michael"

message 2: by Liralen (new) *Mar 08, 2026 10:50AM* "You have a user page, not an author page. Moved to a new author page here: https://www.goodreads.com/author/show... To claim the page, please scroll down and click the link for 'Is this you? Let us know.'"

message 3: by Michael (new) *Mar 08, 2026 10:53AM* "Awesome! Thank you for responding so quickly!"

message 4: by Michael (new) *8 hours, 15 min ago* "Hi there again, For some reason, my book is attributed to the wrong Michael O'Rourke again. It was corrected a day ago and I claimed the page successfully, but it shows the wrong author again.

https://www.goodreads.com/book/show/2.. (goodreads.com in Bing). Could you please move it to this Michael O'Rourke? https://www.goodreads.com/author/show... Thank you so much for your help! Michael"

Analysis and Interpretation

- Manual corrections may not always persist. In this example, a librarian moved the book to what appeared to be the correct author page, but the change seemed to revert within a day.

- Automated processes may override human adjustments. The reversion in this instance could indicate that Goodreads' cataloging or ingestion processes might reassign books based on name matching or external metadata, even after a manual correction.

- Claiming an author page may not always stabilize attribution. Although the author claimed the newly created page, the book still appeared to return to the earlier profile, suggesting that page claims alone may not prevent reversion.

- Name-based identity collisions may occur for authors who share names. This discussion may reflect how reliance on name matching can contribute to repeated misattribution when multiple authors have similar or identical names.

- Authors may have limited ability to prevent reversion. Based on this exchange, the author did not appear to have a method to stop the reassignment after following the steps provided in the discussion.

Taken together, this incident may illustrate how Goodreads' automated processes could potentially override librarian intervention and author participation. It may also suggest that author identity on the platform can be fragile when multiple individuals share the same name. The rapid reversion in this example could imply that automated ingestion or matching processes were active during this period, creating situations that authors might not be able to resolve on their own.

Context and Overview

This chapter documents a publicly visible discussion in the Goodreads Librarians Group in March 2026. In that exchange, an author reported that their name appeared to have been altered on Goodreads—from "KC Gill" to "K.C. Gill"—a change they stated they did not initiate and could not reverse. This punctuation change seemed to result in two of their books being attributed to a different author with a similar name. The author also mentioned that Amazon Author Central had recently associated another writer's book with their profile.

This incident may illustrate how automated name-formatting or cataloging processes on Goodreads could potentially contribute to identity collisions, which in turn might lead to misattribution. It may also suggest how changes in one part of an interconnected ecosystem could appear to influence attribution elsewhere. The transcript is preserved exactly as it appeared.

Snapshot Transcript (Verbatim)

Goodreads Librarians Group discussion *Book & Author Page Issues > Books attributed to another author 6 views Comments Showing 1–3 of 3 Date: March 2026*

message 1: by K.C. (new) *13 hours, 8 min ago* "Hello, somehow my author name got changed from KC Gill to 'K.C. Gill.' It is not and has never been 'K.C. Gill,' and I'm unable to change it, which has resulted in two of my books being credited to another author. (I also had to remove this other author's book from my Author Central page on Amazon recently because it was somehow accredited to me)

The books in question are:

https://www.goodreads.com/book/show/2...?
https://www.goodreads.com/book/show/2...

Is it possible to get my author name corrected and my books correctly credited?"

message 2: by Emily (new) *12 hours, 55 min ago* "On Goodreads, single letters are given punctuation. Someone at Goodreads changed yours a couple years ago. I have moved your books to your profile and left the others on a different profile. If you'd like to contact Goodreads about the punctuation, here is the link: https://www.goodreads.com/about/conta..." (goodreads.com in Bing)

message 3: by K.C. (new) *2 hours, 33 min ago* "K.C. wrote: 'Hello, somehow my author name got changed from KC Gill to "K.C. Gill." It is not and has never been "K.C. Gill," and I'm unable to change it, which has resulted in two of my books being credited to...' Thank you very much."

Analysis and Interpretation

- Goodreads may automatically punctuate single-letter initials. In this example, the librarian states that the platform applies punctuation rules ("K.C." instead of "KC"), which may reflect how the system formats initials in some cases.

- Internal edits may override an author's preferred name. The author reports that they never used "K.C. Gill," yet their name appears to have been changed "a couple years ago," according to the librarian. This may indicate that name formatting can be adjusted by the system or through earlier edits.

- Name-formatting changes may contribute to misattribution. The shift from "KC Gill" to "K.C. Gill" appears to have resulted in two books being associated with another author who has a similar name.

- Misattribution may occur across platforms. The author notes that Amazon Author Central also associated another writer's book with their profile, which could suggest that similar name-matching challenges arise in multiple cataloging environments.

- Authors may have limited ability to correct their own name formatting. In this discussion, the author is not able to change their displayed name directly and is advised to contact

Goodreads Support, suggesting that authors may rely on staff intervention for identity-related adjustments.

- Librarians may be able to move books but not modify identity rules. The librarian reassigns the books but indicates that name-formatting issues fall outside librarian permissions, which may reflect role limitations within the platform.

Taken together, this incident may illustrate how automated name-standardization practices or earlier edits could contribute to identity instability for authors who use initials. The resulting misattribution may affect multiple platforms, and authors may have limited tools to correct or prevent these issues on their own. This pattern appears consistent with other publicly visible discussions from the same period, where automated processes, name collisions, and limited author control were recurring themes.

Context and Overview

This chapter documents a publicly visible discussion in the Goodreads Librarians Group in March 2026. In that exchange, a librarian and a user attempted to address what appeared to be a misattribution involving two authors with nearly identical names: Thomas A. Miller and Thomas A. Miller MD. A book titled *Did Jesus Really Rise from the Dead?* had been associated with the wrong author profile. Although a librarian marked the issue as resolved, the correction did not seem to take effect immediately, and the author page for the intended writer appeared to disappear temporarily.

This incident may illustrate how Goodreads' name-matching processes could potentially conflate authors with similar names, how corrections might not apply consistently or right away, and how librarian actions may sometimes require multiple attempts to stabilize. The transcript is preserved exactly as it appeared.

Snapshot Transcript (Verbatim)

Goodreads Librarians Group discussion *Book & Author Page Issues > Book attributed to wrong author [done.] 6 views Comments Showing 1–5 of 5 Date: March 7, 2026*

message 1: by Kaylee (new) *Mar 07, 2026 08:55AM* "There are two different authors with almost the same name, Thomas A. Miller, and Thomas A. Miller MD.

On this profile... https://www.goodreads.com/author/list...

The book *Did Jesus Really Rise from the Dead?* was actually written by this author, Thomas A. Miller MD: https://www.goodreads.com/author/show...

Could someone move that book over, please? Just that one book."

message 2: by Scott (new) *Mar 07, 2026 09:30AM* "done"

message 3: by Kaylee (new) *7 hours, 29 min ago* "Scott wrote: 'done'

The book is still attached to the wrong author, and the author page for Thomas A. Miller MD seems to be gone. Did it get deleted? These are two different authors, not the same person."

message 4: by Scott (new) *7 hours, 26 min ago* "Sorry, I misunderstood. I have moved the Jesus book to a new profile."

message 5: by Kaylee (new) *5 hours, 10 min ago* "Thanks, and no worries."

Analysis and Interpretation

- Name similarity may contribute to identity collisions. In this example, Goodreads' reliance on name matching appears to have resulted in books by different authors with nearly identical names being associated with the wrong profile.

- Initial corrections may not always take effect immediately. Although the librarian marked the issue as "done," the book still appeared on the earlier profile, which may indicate that the correction did not apply right away or may have been overwritten by another process.

- Author profiles may temporarily disappear during adjustments. The user noted that the correct author page "seems to be gone," suggesting that profiles might be merged, hidden, or recreated as part of the correction process.

- Multiple correction attempts may be needed. The librarian intervened a second time to resolve the issue, ultimately moving the book to a newly created profile, which may reflect the complexity of resolving name-based conflicts.

- Librarians may rely on manual adjustments when addressing identity issues. The resolution involved creating a new profile rather than restoring the existing one, which could suggest limitations in how identity conflicts can be addressed within the platform.

Taken together, this incident may illustrate how Goodreads' name-matching processes can struggle to differentiate between authors with similar names, potentially leading to misattribution and temporary instability in author profiles. It may also suggest that corrections sometimes require multiple steps and that automated matching or ingestion processes could complicate librarian actions. This pattern appears consistent with other publicly visible discussions in this book, where name-based conflation, identity instability, and repeated manual intervention were recurring themes.

Context and Overview

This chapter documents a publicly visible discussion in the Goodreads Librarians Group spanning from January to March 2026. In that exchange, a user repeatedly attempted to correct the descriptions for several editions of *Enshittification* by Cory Doctorow, including the U.S. hardcover, Kindle edition, and digital audiobook. Although a librarian applied a correction and set a default description, the audiobook edition did not appear to update for nearly two months, despite more than twenty follow-up requests.

This incident may illustrate how Goodreads' metadata-propagation processes could potentially update some editions more quickly than others, even when a librarian intervenes. It may also suggest how authors and readers can experience delays or incomplete corrections when metadata is distributed across multiple formats. The transcript is preserved exactly as it appeared.

Snapshot Transcript (Verbatim)

Goodreads Librarians Group discussion *Book & Author Page Issues > [INCOMPLETE SINCE JANUARY] Description Errors: Enshittification 24 views Comments Showing 1–26 of 26 Date Range: January 11 – March 4, 2026*

message 1: by Drace (new) *Jan 11, 2026 09:55AM* "A few different editions of the book *Enshittification* by Cory Doctorow have incorrect descriptions.

US Hardcover: *Enshittification: Why Everything Suddenly Got Worse and What to Do About It* (ISBN 9780374619329) US Kindle: *Enshittification: Why Everything Suddenly Got Worse and What to Do About It* (ASIN B0DQJ5TWB1) Digital Audiobook: *Enshittification: Why Everything Suddenly Got Worse and What to Do About It* (ISBN 9781250417602)

All of their descriptions need to be changed to the following:

[Full replacement description text provided.]"

message 2: by Drace (new) *Jan 13, 2026 07:45AM* "Bumping."

message 3: by Drace (new) *Jan 15, 2026 07:21AM* "Another bump."

message 4: by Drace (new) *Jan 21, 2026 08:32AM* "Bump."

message 5: by Drace (new) *Jan 23, 2026 11:51AM* "Bumping."

message 6: by Drace (new) *Jan 27, 2026 06:01AM* "Another bump."

message 7: by Drace (new) *Jan 29, 2026 06:33AM* "Bumping again."

message 8: by Drace (new) *Feb 02, 2026 10:35AM* "Bump."

message 9: by Scott (new) *Feb 02, 2026 10:36AM* "Done.."

message 10: by Drace (new) *Feb 02, 2026 11:19AM* "Thank you for your help, but the description still needs to be changed on the digital audiobook."

message 11: by Scott (new) *Feb 02, 2026 11:38AM* "I set it as default. It probably just hasn't changed yet."

message 12: by Drace (new) *Feb 04, 2026 07:28AM* "Bumping. It still hasn't changed on the audiobook."

message 13: by Drace (new) *Feb 06, 2026 09:50AM* "Bump."

message 14: by Drace (new) *Feb 08, 2026 06:10AM* "Another bump."

message 15: by Drace (new) *Feb 10, 2026 06:19AM* "Bumping again for the audiobook."

message 16: by Drace (new) *Feb 12, 2026 09:39AM* "Bump."

message 17: by Drace (new) *Feb 14, 2026 02:10PM* "Another bump."

message 18: by Drace (new) *Feb 18, 2026 05:08AM* "Bumping."

message 19: by Drace (new) *Feb 20, 2026 08:41AM* "Bump once again."

message 20: by Drace (new) *Feb 22, 2026 02:59PM* "Bump."

message 21: by Drace (new) *Feb 24, 2026 07:26AM* "Bumping."

message 22: by Drace (new) *Feb 26, 2026 06:44AM* "Bump."

message 23: by Drace (new) *Feb 28, 2026 03:07PM* "Bump again."

message 24: by Drace (new) *Mar 02, 2026 07:07AM* "Again, bumping to correct the audiobook description."

message 25: by Drace (new) *Mar 04, 2026 06:14AM* "Bump."

message 26: by Drace (new) *21 hours, 4 min ago* "Bumping."

Analysis and Interpretation

- Corrections may not apply uniformly across all editions. In this example, the hardcover and Kindle descriptions appeared to update, while the audiobook description did not change for nearly two months.

- Setting a "default" description may not guarantee propagation. Although the librarian indicated that a default description had been set, the audiobook edition did not appear to reflect the update, which may suggest that propagation can vary by format.

- Metadata propagation delays may be lengthy. The user posted more than twenty follow-up messages over an eight-week period, indicating that some updates may take significant time to appear.

- Librarian intervention may have limited reach. Even after a librarian applied a correction, the affected edition did not update, which could imply that certain metadata fields are influenced by automated ingestion processes or external data sources.

- High-profile titles may still experience inconsistencies. *Enshittification* is a widely discussed book by a well-known author, yet the metadata remained inconsistent across formats, suggesting that visibility or prominence does not necessarily prevent delays.

- Users may rely on repeated "bumps" to keep issues visible. The number of bumps in this discussion may indicate that users feel ongoing reminders are necessary to maintain attention on unresolved issues.

Taken together, this incident may illustrate how Goodreads' metadata processes can sometimes fail to synchronize descriptions across different formats, even when corrections are requested early and repeatedly. It may also suggest that manual librarian actions can be delayed, complicated, or potentially overridden by automated processes, leaving some editions in a prolonged incorrect state. This pattern appears consistent with other chapters in this book, where incomplete corrections, automated overrides, and long delays in metadata updates were recurring themes.

Context and Overview

This chapter documents a publicly visible discussion in the Goodreads Librarians Group from February to March 2026. In that exchange, a user reported four editions of *Nineteen Eighty* that they believed were invalid and needed to be marked accordingly. Over the course of a month, the user posted repeated follow-up messages ("bumps") to keep the issue visible, but no librarian response or correction appeared during that period.

This incident may illustrate how invalid or duplicate editions on Goodreads can remain active for extended periods, even when users clearly identify and repeatedly report the issues. It may also suggest that users sometimes rely on persistent bumping to draw attention to unresolved catalog concerns. The transcript is preserved exactly as it appeared.

Snapshot Transcript (Verbatim)

Goodreads Librarians Group discussion *Book & Author Page Issues > [INCOMPLETE] Four invalid editions 15 views Comments Showing 1–15 of 15 Date Range: February 4 – March 4, 2026*

message 1: by Drace (new) *Feb 04, 2026 07:33AM* "The following editions of the book *Nineteen Eighty* are invalid and need to be marked as such.

1.   https://www.goodreads.com/book/show/1...

2.   https://www.goodreads.com/book/show/1...

3.   https://www.goodreads.com/book/show/1...

4.   https://www.goodreads.com/book/show/5..."

message 2: by Drace (new) *Feb 06, 2026 12:08PM* "Bumping."

message 3: by Drace (new) *Feb 08, 2026 11:13AM* "Another bump."

message 4: by Drace (new) *Feb 10, 2026 06:16AM* "Bump."

message 5: by Drace (new) *Feb 12, 2026 09:39AM* "Bump again."

message 6: by Drace (new) *Feb 14, 2026 02:10PM* "Another bump."

message 7: by Drace (new) *Feb 18, 2026 05:07AM* "Bumping."

message 8: by Drace (new) *Feb 20, 2026 08:40AM* "Bump."

message 9: by Drace (new) *Feb 22, 2026 02:58PM* "Bump once again."

message 10: by Drace (new) *Feb 24, 2026 07:23AM* "Bumping."

message 11: by Drace (new) *Feb 26, 2026 06:43AM* "Bump."

message 12: by Drace (new) *Feb 28, 2026 03:06PM* "Another bump."

message 13: by Drace (new) *Mar 02, 2026 07:05AM* "Bumping again."

message 14: by Drace (new) *Mar 04, 2026 06:11AM* "Bumping."

message 15: by Drace (new) *21 hours, 4 min ago* "Bump."

Analysis and Interpretation

- Invalid editions may remain active for extended periods. In this example, the four editions identified by the user as invalid did not appear to be updated or marked over the course of a month.

- No librarian response may occur in some cases. Unlike other discussions where librarians eventually intervened, this thread did not receive replies during the period shown, leaving the reported issue unresolved.

- Users may rely on repeated bumps to maintain visibility. The user posted more than a dozen bumps, which may indicate that unresolved issues can fall out of view without continued reminders.

- Edition cleanup may be deprioritized or delayed. Even when invalid editions are explicitly listed, corrections may not be applied promptly, based on what is visible in this discussion.

- Automated detection for invalid or duplicate editions may be limited. The need for manual reporting—and the absence of a visible response—could suggest that Goodreads does not automatically identify or retire entries that users consider invalid.

- Catalog integrity may depend heavily on volunteer action. Without librarian intervention, the editions in question remained part of the public record throughout the period documented.

Taken together, this incident may illustrate how Goodreads' edition-management processes can leave incorrect or duplicate editions unaddressed, even when users provide clear evidence and repeated reminders. This pattern appears consistent with other chapters in this book, where incomplete corrections, long delays, and reliance on manual intervention were recurring themes.

Context and Overview

This chapter documents a publicly visible discussion in the Goodreads Librarians Group from February to March 2026. In that exchange, a user reported what they believed were multiple incorrect publication dates for the novel *Backmask*, including discrepancies between the ebook, Kindle edition, and the work's original publication date. The user stated that the correct date—June 13, 2023—was confirmed by the publisher's website, yet Goodreads displayed conflicting dates across editions and did not list the original publication date.

Despite repeated follow-up messages over several weeks, no librarian response or visible correction occurred during the period shown. This incident may illustrate how Goodreads' date-handling processes could leave inconsistent metadata in place for extended periods, even when users provide what they consider authoritative sources. The transcript is preserved exactly as it appeared.

Snapshot Transcript (Verbatim)

Goodreads Librarians Group discussion *Book & Author Page Issues >
[INCOMPLETE] Date Issues: Backmask 12 views Comments Showing 1–12
of 12 Date Range: February 10 – March 4, 2026*

message 1: by Drace (new) *Feb 10, 2026 07:34AM* "There are a few issues with dates to clean up on the novel *Backmask*.

The publisher's site confirms in multiple places that the publication date was June 13, 2023: https://malarkeybooks.com/backmask // https://malarkeybooks.com/catalogue (Ctrl+F the title on the second link).

Backmask – Ebook edition, ISBN 9781088102732 – The date is incorrectly set to June 13 2024. It needs to be 2023.

Backmask – Kindle edition, ASIN B0C5KC13H1 – This edition's date is set to May 23 2023, and the Amazon page says the same, but I believe this might be a case where the Kindle page was created before release and the date never corrected. Since the publisher site lists the June date as the publication date, I believe this edition's date should be changed to match.

https://www.goodreads.com/work/editio... – All Editions – the Original Publication Date is missing and needs to be set to June 13 2023."

message 2: by Drace (new) *Feb 12, 2026 09:38AM* "Bumping."

message 3: by Drace (new) *Feb 14, 2026 02:09PM* "Bump."

message 4: by Drace (new) *Feb 18, 2026 05:06AM* "Bump again."

message 5: by Drace (new) *Feb 20, 2026 08:39AM* "Bumping."

message 6: by Drace (new) *Feb 22, 2026 02:57PM* "Bump."

message 7: by Drace (new) *Feb 24, 2026 07:23AM* "Another bump."

message 8: by Drace (new) *Feb 26, 2026 06:43AM* "Bumping."

message 9: by Drace (new) *Feb 28, 2026 03:06PM* "Bump again."

message 10: by Drace (new) *Mar 02, 2026 07:05AM* "Bump."

message 11: by Drace (new) *Mar 04, 2026 06:11AM* "Bumping."

message 12: by Drace (new) *21 hours, 5 min ago* "Bump again."

Analysis and Interpretation

- Conflicting dates across editions may remain unresolved. In this example, the ebook, Kindle edition, and work record all displayed different dates, none of which matched the date the user identified from the publisher's website.

- Original publication date fields may remain blank for extended periods. Even when the user provided what they considered an authoritative source, the "Original Publication Date" field did not appear to update.

- No librarian response may occur in some cases. Unlike other discussions where librarians eventually intervened, this thread did not receive replies during the period shown.

- Users may rely on repeated bumps to maintain visibility. The user posted more than ten bumps, which may indicate that unresolved metadata issues can fall out of view without continued reminders.

- Date corrections may require manual intervention. Goodreads did not appear to reconcile the conflicting dates automatically, even when the discrepancies were clearly identified.

- Automated ingestion may influence or complicate corrections. The Kindle edition's date appeared to reflect Amazon's listing rather than the publisher's confirmed release date, which could suggest that external metadata feeds play a role in how dates are displayed.

Taken together, this incident may illustrate how Goodreads' date-handling processes can leave incorrect or conflicting publication dates in place for extended periods, even when users provide detailed explanations and sources they consider authoritative. This pattern appears consistent with other chapters in this book, where incomplete corrections, lack of response, and reliance on manual intervention were recurring themes.

Chapter Eight — Multi-Issue Metadata Errors Remaining Unresolved for Months (December 2025 – March 2026)

Context and Overview

This chapter documents a publicly visible discussion in the Goodreads Librarians Group from December 2025 through March 2026. In that exchange, a user reported numerous metadata issues affecting two volumes of *I Feel You Linger in the Air*, including what they described as incorrect descriptions, missing page counts, uncombined editions, missing contributor information, and misattributed authors. Although some issues related to Volume 1 appeared to receive partial attention, most of the reported problems remained unresolved for months, prompting the user to post repeated follow-up messages.

This incident may illustrate how complex metadata issues—particularly those involving multiple editions, translations, and contributor roles—can remain incomplete for extended periods. It may also suggest limitations in librarian permissions, the impact of broader system-wide outages (such as combining being temporarily disabled), and the persistence of author-identity inconsistencies. The transcript is preserved exactly as it appeared.

Snapshot Transcript (Verbatim)

Goodreads Librarians Group discussion *Book & Author Page Issues > (OPEN since 12/07) Fix/Add Missing Informations (I Feel You Linger in the Air Vol.1 and 2) 27 views Comments Showing 1–14 of 14 Date Range: December 7, 2025 – March 1, 2026*

message 1: by Sara (new) *Dec 07, 2025 07:06AM (last edited Dec 28, 2025 07:05AM)* "Hi, I want to make a request to fix/add missing informations about the 2 volumes of this series, in the first one the description and page count are wrong, in the second an edition isn't combined and the other doesn't have format nor page count. Also, I noticed that the paperback editions for the first (Italian and Vietnamese) and second volume (Italian) redirect you to another author with the same name.

12/28 edit: The Vol. 1 parts of the request are already answered (except for the part of the 'fake' author).

Vol. 1 Page count source (for the paperback): https://www.goodreads.com/photo/user/... Description (Paperback/Kindle): [Jom/architect Italian description text] Source (Publisher's site): https://www.kitsunelab.it/product/fee... Book (Paperback): https://www.goodreads.com/book/show/2... — ISBN: 9791298507401 Book (Kindle): https://www.goodreads.com/book/show/2... — ISBN: 9791298507418

Vol. 2 Book (Kindle): https://www.goodreads.com/book/show/2... — ISBN: 9791298507494 Combine with: https://www.goodreads.com/book/show/1... — ASIN: B0DM4KDHK7 Book (Paperback — listed as 'unknown binding'): https://www.goodreads.com/book/show/2... — ISBN: 9791298507463 Page count source (book in hand): https://www.goodreads.com/photo/user/... Translator and revisers: https://www.goodreads.com/photo/user/... Translator is Alessia Ratti.

The real author for the editions I mentioned at the start of the request is this: https://www.goodreads.com/author/show...

The book pages that redirect you to the wrong one are: https://www.goodreads.com/book/show/2... https://www.goodreads.com/book/show/1... https://www.goodreads.com/book/show/2..."

message 2: by Sara (new) *Dec 14, 2025 02:22PM* "Bump"

message 3: by Sara (new) *Dec 21, 2025 11:50AM* "Bump"

message 4: by Livietta (new) *Dec 25, 2025 11:31PM* "Translator reviewer are not listed as standard contributor. Combining is temporary unavailable until january."

message 5: by Sara (new) *Jan 04, 2026 11:27AM* "Bump"

message 6: by Sara (new) *Jan 12, 2026 01:49PM* "Bump"

message 7: by Sara (new) *Jan 18, 2026 10:53AM* "Bump"

message 8: by Sara (new) *Jan 25, 2026 07:40AM* "Bump"

message 9: by Sara (new) *Feb 01, 2026 07:31AM* "Bump"

message 10: by Sara (new) *Feb 08, 2026 08:48AM* "Bump"

message 11: by Sara (new) *Feb 15, 2026 01:03PM* "Bump"

message 12: by Sara (new) *Feb 22, 2026 06:18AM* "Bump"

message 13: by Sara (new) *Mar 01, 2026 02:03PM* "Bump"

message 14: by Sara (new) *22 hours, 57 min ago* "Bump"

Analysis and Interpretation

- Large, multi-issue requests may remain unresolved for long periods. In this example, most of the reported problems stayed open from December through March, despite detailed documentation and repeated bumps.

- Edition-combining outages may halt progress. A librarian noted that combining was "temporarily unavailable until January," which may have prevented certain corrections for Volume 2.

- Contributor roles may be limited by system rules. The user attempted to add translators and revisers, but the librarian indicated that Goodreads does not treat those roles as standard contributor types, which may restrict how they can be recorded.

- Author misattribution may persist across multiple editions. Several paperback editions appeared to redirect to the wrong author, and this issue remained unresolved even after other fixes were applied.

- Metadata inconsistencies may span multiple fields. The request involved incorrect descriptions, missing page counts, missing formats, uncombined editions, missing contributors, incorrect author attribution, multiple ISBNs and ASINs, and cross-language editions. This level of complexity may exceed what librarians can easily resolve manually.

- Users may rely on persistent bumps to keep issues visible. The user bumped the thread more than a dozen times over three months, suggesting that ongoing reminders may be necessary to maintain visibility.

- Partial fixes may not resolve underlying issues. Some corrections were applied to Volume 1, but the broader author-identity problem appeared to remain.

Taken together, this incident may illustrate how Goodreads' metadata processes can struggle with multi-edition, multi-language, and multi-format works—particularly when corrections require combining, contributor additions, or adjustments to author identity. It may also suggest that system limitations and temporary feature outages can leave complex requests incomplete for extended periods. This pattern appears consistent with other chapters in this book, where incomplete corrections, long delays, and persistent identity inconsistencies were recurring themes.

Context and Overview

This chapter documents a publicly visible discussion in the Goodreads Librarians Group from February to March 2026. In that exchange, a user asked that a Serbian edition of *Romeo and Juliet* (ISBN 978-86-17-17999-9) be added and combined with the main work record. They also requested that the page count be added and that the blurry cover be replaced with a clearer version from the publisher. Despite the straightforward nature of the request and the global prominence of the underlying work, the thread received no librarian responses. The user continued to bump the request for nearly three weeks without visible progress.

This incident may illustrate how even widely recognized, high-profile works can experience metadata stagnation on Goodreads. It may also suggest that edition combining—a core function of the platform—can remain unaddressed for extended periods, even when users provide complete information and clear sources. The transcript is preserved exactly as it appeared.

Snapshot Transcript (Verbatim)

Goodreads Librarians Group discussion *Book & Author Page Issues >* *[OPEN] Please combine This topic is about Romeo and Juliet 15 views* *Comments Showing 1–6 of 6 Date Range: February 18 – March 8, 2026*

message 1: by Lidija (new) *Feb 18, 2026 01:06PM (last edited Feb 18, 2026 01:25PM)* "This book 978-86-17-17999-9 is just the Serbian version of *Romeo and Juliette* … can you please add it? Vilijan Sekspir is the Serbian writing for Shakespeare.. thanks.

Can you also add pages.. here is the link from the publisher: https://www.knjizara.zavod.co.rs/rome... 147 pages.

If it's not too much to ask it would be nice to replace the cover as well since it's soo blurryy."

message 2: by Lidija (new) *Feb 21, 2026 11:54AM* "Up"

message 3: by Lidija (new) *Feb 28, 2026 05:30AM* "up"

message 4: by Lidija (new) *Mar 01, 2026 05:42AM* "up"

message 5: by Lidija (new) *Mar 05, 2026 05:22AM* "up"

message 6: by Lidija (new) *Mar 08, 2026 11:55AM* "Up"

Analysis and Interpretation

- Even globally recognized works may experience metadata stagnation. *Romeo and Juliet* is one of the most widely cataloged works in literary history, yet this straightforward request to add and combine a single Serbian edition remained unanswered for nearly three weeks.

- Some threads may receive no librarian response. In this case, the request saw no replies at all, leaving the edition uncombined, the page count unadded, and the cover unreplaced.

- Users may rely on repeated bumps to maintain visibility. The user bumped the thread five times, which may indicate that unresolved issues can otherwise fall out of view in the queue.

- Edition combining may function as a bottleneck. Combining is one of the most common librarian tasks, yet this request— simple, well-documented, and involving a canonical work— remained open, suggesting that combining may be backlogged, deprioritized, or affected by system constraints.

- Metadata corrections may depend entirely on manual intervention. Adding page counts, replacing covers, and combining editions do not appear to be automated processes, meaning that progress relies on volunteer availability.

- Non-Latin scripts and transliterations may complicate matching. The Serbian transliteration "Vilijan Sekspir" may not automatically match "William Shakespeare," potentially requiring manual linking by a librarian.

Taken together, this incident may illustrate how Goodreads' metadata processes can struggle not only with obscure or independently published works but also with universally recognized classics. The lack of response may suggest that edition combining is subject to delays, backlogs, or system limitations. This pattern appears consistent with other chapters in this book, where incomplete corrections, long delays, and reliance on repeated user bumps were recurring themes.

Context and Overview

This chapter documents a publicly visible discussion in the Goodreads Librarians Group in March 2026. In that exchange, a self-published author attempted to add their newly released book to Goodreads and link it to their author profile. They reported using the "Is this you?" claim link multiple times, but the claim did not appear to succeed. Shortly afterward, the author noticed that their displayed name on Goodreads had changed from their full legal name, *Prince Marlo Delicano Montadas*, to *Marlo Montadas*—a change they stated they did not initiate and could not reverse.

The responding librarian explained that Goodreads does not include "titles" in author names, but the author clarified that *Prince* is part of their given name rather than an honorific. The librarian expressed uncertainty about how Goodreads handles such cases, suggesting that the platform's naming conventions may not fully account for certain cultural naming structures.

Snapshot Transcript (Verbatim)

Goodreads Librarians Group discussion *Book & Author Page Issues > Please Add My Book to My Author Profile and Include the Book Description 8 views Comments Showing 1–9 of 9 Date: March 7–8, 2026*

message 1: by Marlo (new) *Mar 07, 2026 06:22PM* "I am a self-published author and recently added my book through the 'Adding New Books and Editions' section.

I already used the 'Is this you? Let us know.' link at the bottom of the profile, but it was unsuccessful twice.

My book appeared on Goodreads today, possibly after I added the Amazon link when it was just published. However, the book description I submitted is missing.

Could you please add the description to the book and link the book to my author profile?

Thank you.

This is my book: https://www.goodreads.com/book/show/2... This is my profile: https://www.goodreads.com/user/show/1...”

message 2: by Scott (new) *Mar 08, 2026 08:01AM* “You need to apply for the profile. Volunteer users cannot make you an author. If you are having problems, contact support.”

message 3: by Marlo (new) *Mar 08, 2026 08:16AM* “Good day, Sir. I applied again earlier today. I can now search for my book using its title; however, I just noticed that the author's name has been changed. My full name is Prince Marlo Delicano Montadas, but it appears as Marlo Montadas on my book listing.

May I kindly ask what might be the reason for this change? I would greatly appreciate any help you could provide regarding this matter.

Thank you very much.”

message 4: by Scott (new) *Mar 08, 2026 08:19AM* “The name must match what is on the book, and we do not include titles.”

message 5: by Marlo (new) *Mar 08, 2026 08:25AM* “I understand, Sir. However, my middle name was included in Amazon, which might have been the reason for the discrepancy.

I am also fine with the name that appears on the book, as it is the name I expect and prefer. My concern is that if the name on the book is correct, why has the author's name been changed to ‘Marlo Montadas’ instead of ‘Prince Marlo Montadas’ when I searched for it?

I truly appreciate your patience and assistance, Sir. Thank you very much.”

message 6: by Scott (new) *Mar 08, 2026 08:28AM* “As I said we do not include titles. Or is ‘Prince’ actually a part of your name, like the musician?”

message 7: by Marlo (new) *Mar 08, 2026 08:35AM* “I apologize for the confusion. Yes, ‘Prince’ is actually part of my name; my given name is Prince Marlo. In our country, it is quite common to include ‘Prince’ or

'Princess' before what is technically the second name. I hope this clarifies the matter. Thank you."

message 8: by Scott (new) *Mar 08, 2026 08:36AM* "Hm, I'm not sure how we would handle that here."

message 9: by Marlo (new) *Mar 08, 2026 08:42AM* "I see. Earlier today it was still correct, but just a few hours ago it was changed to 'Marlo Montadas.' Unfortunately, there's nothing I can do about it from my end, so I'm simply raising the concern. I hope it can be fixed at some point. Thank you very much, and have a great day!"

Analysis and Interpretation

- Author claims may fail repeatedly. The author attempted to claim their profile multiple times without success, leaving them unable to link their new book or manage their displayed identity.

- Author names may be altered without the author initiating the change. The author reported that their full legal name was shortened to "Marlo Montadas," removing both the given name *Prince* and the middle names.

- Internal naming rules may not align with global naming conventions. The librarian initially assumed "Prince" was a title rather than part of the author's given name, which may reflect how the system interprets certain name structures.

- Automated ingestion or background processes may overwrite user-submitted metadata. The author noted that their name appeared correctly earlier in the day but changed "a few hours ago," which could suggest that an automated update replaced the original entry.

- Librarians may lack clarity on non-Western naming structures. The librarian expressed uncertainty about how Goodreads handles names like "Prince Marlo," indicating that guidance or flexibility may be limited.

- Authors may not be able to correct their own names. Goodreads does not allow authors to edit their author-page names directly, leaving them dependent on support staff for identity corrections.

- Book descriptions submitted during the addition process may not appear. The author's description did not show up on the listing, even though they submitted it when adding the book.

Taken together, this incident may illustrate how Goodreads' identity-handling practices and automated metadata processes can override author intent, particularly for authors whose naming conventions fall outside the platform's assumptions. It may also suggest that new authors can struggle to establish or correct their identity on the platform, even when they provide accurate information and follow the recommended steps. This pattern appears consistent with other chapters in this book, where identity instability, metadata overrides, and limited author control recur across multiple cases.

Chapter Eleven — Duplicate Author Profiles Remaining Unresolved for Two Months (January–March 2026)

Context and Overview

This chapter documents a publicly visible discussion in the Goodreads Librarians Group from January to March 2026. In that exchange, a user reported that an author appeared to have been duplicated on Goodreads, resulting in two separate author profiles for the same individual. The user also noted that one of the author's books had been split between the two profiles and needed to be combined with the correct edition. Despite the clarity and simplicity of the request, the thread received no librarian responses for two months. The user continued to follow up at regular intervals, but the duplicate profile and split book entry remained unchanged throughout the period shown.

This incident may illustrate how duplicate author profiles can remain active on Goodreads for extended periods, even when the issue is clearly documented and repeatedly reported. It may also suggest that identity corrections depend heavily on manual librarian intervention and that the platform may not have automated safeguards to detect or prevent duplicate author creation. The transcript is preserved exactly as it appeared.

Snapshot Transcript (Verbatim)

Goodreads Librarians Group discussion *Book & Author Page Issues > [Open] Duplicated author 13 views Comments Showing 1–7 of 7 Date Range: January 7 – March 7, 2026*

message 1: by Ilie (new) *Jan 07, 2026 11:45PM* "Hello,

This author https://www.goodreads.com/author/show... is a duplication of this author https://www.goodreads.com/author/show...

In addition, his book https://www.goodreads.com/book/show/1... should be combined with the original one https://www.goodreads.com/book/show/5...

Can a Librarian please help? Thanks!"

message 2: by Ilie (new) *Jan 17, 2026 01:44AM* "Can a Librarian please check this request? Thanks"

message 3: by Ilie (new) *Jan 27, 2026 10:19AM* "Can a Librarian please check this request? Thanks"

message 4: by Ilie (new) *Feb 07, 2026 11:23PM* "Can a Librarian please check this request? Thanks"

message 5: by Ilie (new) *Feb 18, 2026 01:48AM* "Can a Librarian please check this request? Thanks"

message 6: by Ilie (new) *Feb 27, 2026 08:43AM* "Can a Librarian please check this request? Thanks"

message 7: by Ilie (new) *Mar 07, 2026 10:42PM* "Can a Librarian please check this request? Thanks"

Analysis and Interpretation

- Duplicate author profiles may remain active for long periods. Even when a user clearly identifies a duplicate and provides direct links, the profiles did not appear to merge or receive flags automatically.

- Some threads may receive no librarian response for extended stretches. Over two months, the user posted seven follow-up messages without acknowledgment or visible action.

- Books may be split across duplicate profiles. One of the author's books appeared under the wrong profile, requiring manual combination with the correct edition.

- Identity corrections may depend entirely on manual intervention. Goodreads did not appear to detect or reconcile the duplicate author entries automatically, even though the names and works matched.

- Users may rely on repeated reminders to keep issues visible. The user bumped the thread at regular intervals, suggesting that unresolved identity issues can otherwise fall out of view.

- Duplicate profiles may distort an author's public presence. When books and editions are divided between multiple profiles, readers may see incomplete or inconsistent bibliographies.

Taken together, this incident may illustrate how Goodreads' author-identity processes can leave duplicate profiles unaddressed, even when users provide clear evidence and repeated reminders. The lack of response may suggest that identity corrections are subject to backlogs, deprioritization, or system limitations. This pattern appears consistent with other chapters in this book, where identity instability, incomplete corrections, and reliance on repeated bumps recur across multiple cases.

Context and Overview

This chapter documents a publicly visible discussion in the Goodreads Librarians Group in March 2026. In that exchange, a user asked that a book be removed because its Amazon link was no longer available. The responding librarian explained that Goodreads does not remove books solely because an Amazon listing disappears. The user then attempted to update the Amazon link and the cover image, but the librarian noted that the ASIN the user provided was already associated with a different book record, creating confusion about which edition the link belonged to.

This incident may illustrate how Goodreads' edition-linking practices rely heavily on ASINs and how users can encounter complications when multiple ASINs exist for the same title. It may also suggest that Goodreads maintains a strict approach to book removal, keeping catalog entries even when the original Amazon listing is no longer active. The transcript is preserved exactly as it appeared.

Snapshot Transcript (Verbatim)

Goodreads Librarians Group discussion *Book & Author Page Issues > Please remove this book This topic is about Cuentos mágicos del universo 13 views Comments Showing 1–7 of 7 Date: March 1–7, 2026*

message 1: by Carla (new) *Mar 01, 2026 03:04PM* "This book link is no longer available in Amazon. Thank you"

message 2: by Scott (new) *Mar 01, 2026 03:06PM* "We don't remove books just because they aren't on Amazon any more."

message 3: by Carla (new) *Mar 04, 2026 02:34PM* "Could you update the link to this one: https://www.amazon.com/es/dp/B0GQ6PM1FJ/ I would also like to update the cover to the one shown on Amazon, but I don't know where to upload it. Thank you"

message 4: by Scott (new) *Mar 04, 2026 03:09PM* "That ASIN is already here."

message 5: by Carla (new) *Mar 05, 2026 03:23PM* "The old ASIN is BO9LSRR4KZ, but the new one I want to change to is BOGQ6PM1FJ."

message 6: by Scott (new) *Mar 06, 2026 07:09AM* "And if you'll search that ASIN you'll find it is already on a book record."

message 7: by Carla (new) *Mar 07, 2026 02:09PM* "Well, I think it's fine that both ASIN are currently listed. Thank you for your time."

Analysis and Interpretation

- Goodreads does not remove books when Amazon links disappear. The platform appears to treat catalog entries as permanent records, regardless of Amazon availability.

- ASINs may determine edition identity. The librarian's responses focused entirely on ASIN matching, suggesting that Goodreads relies heavily on Amazon identifiers to link or separate editions.

- Multiple ASINs for the same title may create confusion. The user attempted to replace an outdated ASIN with a new one, but Goodreads treated them as separate editions rather than updates.

- Users cannot update covers directly. Goodreads does not allow authors or readers to upload covers for many editions, leaving them dependent on librarians or automated ingestion.

- Librarian responses may be brief and procedural. The librarian did not explain why the ASIN could not be updated or how the system determines edition identity, leaving the user to infer that having both ASINs listed was acceptable.

- Edition fragmentation may persist when ASINs change. When Amazon replaces or retires an ASIN, Goodreads may retain the old one indefinitely, resulting in multiple parallel editions.

This incident possibly demonstrates how Goodreads' reliance on ASINs and its strict no-removal policy can lead to persistent edition fragmentation and user confusion. The pattern aligns with other chapters in this book: metadata rigidity, limited user control, and the difficulty of correcting or updating edition information once it has been ingested.

Context and Overview

This chapter documents a publicly visible discussion in the Goodreads Librarians Group from February to March 2026. A new member discovered that Goodreads had already created an author profile for him, containing several works — including one he did not write and two unpublished manuscripts that had been privately circulated. He attempted to claim the existing profile but encountered repeated errors, including a requirement to provide publisher information he did not yet have.

Over the following month, the author attempted to correct misattributed works, remove invalid entries, and complete the author claim process. Although librarians were able to mark the unpublished manuscripts invalid and remove the misattributed book, they repeatedly directed the author to contact Goodreads Support for all issues related to the author program. The author was unable to reapply because the "Is this you?" link disappeared after his first attempt.

This incident possibly illustrates how Goodreads' identity-handling system can surface or create author profiles containing misattributed and unpublished works, while simultaneously preventing authors from successfully claiming their own pages. It also possibly highlights the limitations of librarian permissions and the lack of a clear pathway for reapplying to the Author Program once an initial attempt has been submitted. The transcript is preserved exactly as it appeared.

Snapshot Transcript (Verbatim)

Goodreads Librarians Group discussion *Book & Author Page Issues > new member dealing with 20 views Comments Showing 1–13 of 13 Date Range: February 5 – March 7, 2026*

message 1: by Max (new) *Feb 05, 2026 07:41PM* "I have just created this profile, and afterward I realized that someone else had already created one for me: https://www.goodreads.com/author/show... That profile includes four books, three of which I wrote. The fourth (https://www.goodreads.com/book/show/1...) is apparently by someone else with the same name. How can I merge the two profiles? How can I separate the book I didn't write from my profile? Thank you for your help. Max Gutmann"

message 2: by Shim (new) *Feb 05, 2026 08:20PM* "You can claim the page using the link at the bottom where it says 'Is this you? Let us know.' You can find more information about the Goodreads Author program here. In that form you can indicate which books do not belong to you and they should get moved."

message 3: by Max (new) *Feb 06, 2026 09:43AM* "Thank you, Shim. I'm in the process of negotiating with a new publisher. So, since I keep getting the message 'Please complete the entire form to identify yourself and/or verify that you have entered a valid email address.' when 'Submit application' to claim my page without publisher information, I suppose I will have to wait until my relationship with this publisher is official. (I'm only mentioning this so that, when I come back to complete this process, Goodreads volunteers won't think I have in the meanwhile simply been ignoring this.) Thank you for your help."

message 4: by Max (new) *Mar 01, 2026 11:39AM* "Regarding updating the page, two of the books listed (Book 58161855: *The Hearthside Treasury of Light and Comic Verse* and Book 60756738: *The Legacy*) are unpublished manuscripts which were circulated privately. Can 'unpublished manuscript' be added in parentheses after their titles? Also, I assume that until my forthcoming book appears on my new publisher's website, I can list the publisher but should just leave the website info blank."

message 5: by Scott (new) *Mar 01, 2026 11:49AM* "I have marked those two works invalid. They should never have been added. Librarians cannot comment on what staff will accept on your application. Please ask them directly for anything to do with the author program."

message 6: by Max (new) *Mar 01, 2026 04:40PM* "Thank you, Scott. How do I contact the staff? (On seeing your message, I tried to submit my page, but I continue to be told it is incomplete.)"

message 7: by Shim (new) *Mar 01, 2026 07:24PM*
https://www.goodreads.com/about/contact

message 8: by Max (new) *Mar 02, 2026 11:41AM* "Thank you, Shim! I wrote to the staff and (I think) got quick help. I do have more questions.

1. Can you verify that I now have ownership of my author page? (And tell me how/where I can see that?)

2. How do make clear that I did not write *The Elder-Beerman Stores Corp: A tradition of success*? When submitting my information, I said the page needed editing and made a point of not selecting that book as among the ones I wrote, but it appears to still be listed on my page."

message 9: by Scott (new) *Mar 02, 2026 12:39PM* "Your author claim has not yet been completed. You can see that your own profile is not an author profile. I've moved the Elder-Beerman book."

message 10: by Max (new) *Mar 02, 2026 02:55PM* "Thank you, Scott! Do I now wait? If there's anything further I need to do to claim my author page, please let me know."

message 11: by Scott (new) *Mar 02, 2026 02:56PM* "Please contact support with any questions about your author account."

message 12: by Max (new) *Mar 06, 2026 05:52PM* "I now have the information that was missing the first time I applied for the author program and trying to reapply. The instructions that I find for applying tell me to scroll down to the bottom of my profile pages and 'Click "Is this you? Let us know!"' But I no longer see the 'Is this you?' presumably because I already clicked on it and told Goodreads it was me the first time I applied. Please advise: in this situation, how do I reapply for the author program? Thank you for your help."

message 13: by Scott (new) *Mar 07, 2026 06:36AM* "Please contact support with any questions about your author account."

Analysis and Interpretation

- Duplicate author profiles may be created automatically. Goodreads had already generated an author page for the user before he created his own account.

- Misattributed works may appear on automatically generated profiles. One book belonged to a different author with the same name.

- Unpublished manuscripts may be added to Goodreads without the author's consent. Two privately circulated works appeared on the author's page and had to be marked invalid.

- Author claims may fail due to missing publisher information. The system required publisher verification even though the author was between publishers.

- Once the "Is this you?" link is used, it may disappear. The author could not reapply after his first attempt, leaving him unable to complete the process.

- Librarians may be unable to assist with author-program issues. All questions about claiming, reapplying, or verifying author status were redirected to Goodreads Support.

- Identity corrections may depend on staff intervention rather than librarians. Librarians could remove invalid works and misattributed books but could not help with the core identity problem.

- The author may have no visibility into the status of his claim. He repeatedly asked whether he had ownership of his author page, but librarians could not confirm.

This incident possibly demonstrates how Goodreads' identity-handling system can create duplicate profiles, misattribute works, and block authors from claiming their own pages — even when they follow the documented steps. It also possibly shows how the disappearance of the "Is this you?" link can trap authors in an incomplete application state, requiring staff intervention to resolve. The pattern aligns with other chapters in this book: identity instability, misattribution, incomplete corrections, and limited author control.

Context and Overview

This chapter documents a publicly visible discussion in the Goodreads Librarians Group in March 2026. A new author, Grace P. S., reported that her debut novel had been automatically linked to a generic "Grace" author profile shared by multiple unrelated writers. She requested that the book be moved to her correct author identity, but librarians explained that they cannot connect books to user profiles and that she must instead claim her author page through the Goodreads Author Program.

The author attempted to use the "Is this you?" claim link but encountered errors, including the system refusing her email address. She then asked for manual intervention, but librarians reiterated that they have no ability to modify author-program status or connect user accounts to author pages. The thread ended without resolution.

This incident possibly illustrates how Goodreads' identity-matching system can misassign books to generic or shared author names, how new authors may struggle to claim their profiles, and how librarians are limited in their ability to correct identity-related issues. The transcript is preserved exactly as it appeared.

Snapshot Transcript (Verbatim)

Goodreads Librarians Group discussion *Book & Author Page Issues > Book Linked to Wrong Author Profile 8 views Comments Showing 1–9 of 9 Date Range: March 3–6, 2026*

message 1: by Grace (new) *Mar 03, 2026 03:55PM* "Hi Librarians, My book is currently linked to the wrong author profile named 'Grace.' This profile does not belong to me. Book title: *The Crimson Orchid: Legacy of the Mirror Throne* Incorrect author profile link: https://www.goodreads.com/author/show... Correct author name: Grace P. S. Correct author profile link: https://www.goodreads.com/book/show/2... I kindly request that my book be unlinked from the incorrect profile and attached to my official author profile. Thank you very much for your help. Best regards, Grace P. S."

message 2: by Scott (new) *Mar 03, 2026 04:07PM* "Is this your only book?"

message 3: by Grace (new) *Mar 03, 2026 08:52PM (last edited Mar 03, 2026 08:59PM)* "I have written other stories in this world, and this is the first published book. I'm planning to continue the series and hope readers will enjoy it."

message 4: by Scott (new) *Mar 05, 2026 07:05AM* "I have moved it to a new profile: https://www.goodreads.com/author/show..."

message 5: by Grace (new) *Mar 06, 2026 04:01AM* "Thank you for trying to help. Unfortunately the book is still linked to the wrong Grace profile. I have contacted the Goodreads librarians to attach it to my correct author profile. I really appreciate your help."

message 6: by Shim (new) *Mar 06, 2026 06:37AM (last edited Mar 06, 2026 06:43AM)* "You must claim the page using the link at the bottom where it says 'Is this you? Let us know.' You can find more information about the Goodreads Author program here. Goodreads Librarians cannot connect user profiles to author pages. If you run into any issues claiming your account, please reach out to Goodreads Support. Goodreads Librarians are not involved in this process and have no way to resolve issues related to claiming accounts."

message 7: by Grace (new) *Mar 06, 2026 08:13AM* "Hello Librarians, I am the author of the book *The Crimson Orchid: Legacy of the Mirror Throne*. Currently, my book is linked to a general profile named 'Grace', which belongs to several other authors. I am a different author and I would like to have my book moved to a separate, correct profile under the name Grace P S. I am unable to use the automated 'Author Program' form as it's not accepting my email address, so I am requesting manual help. Details for the move: Book Title: *The Crimson Orchid: Legacy of the Mirror Throne* Author Name as it appears now: Grace Author Name I want to use: Grace P S My Contact Email: [email address] Amazon Book Link: javascript:void(0) Please move this book to a new profile for me. Thank you for your assistance. Regards, Grace P S" message 8: by Scott (new) *Mar 06, 2026 08:19AM* "If you are having trouble with the author program, you need to contact support."

message 9: by Shim (new) *Mar 06, 2026 09:31AM (last edited Mar 06, 2026 09:31AM)* "I don't recommend posting your email address here, as this is a public forum. There is no manual option here for Librarians to assist you with. Editing privileges for Librarians are limited by Goodreads."

Analysis and Interpretation

- Books may be linked to generic or shared author profiles. The author's debut novel was automatically assigned to a generic "Grace" profile used by multiple unrelated writers.

- Librarians may be able to move books between author profiles but cannot link them to user accounts. The librarian created a new author profile, but the book remained attached to the wrong one because only Goodreads staff can connect a book to a user-owned author page.

- The Author Program may be the only pathway to claim identity. Librarians repeatedly emphasized that they cannot manually attach books to user profiles.

- The author-claim form may reject valid email addresses. The author reported that the system would not accept her email, blocking her from completing the claim.

- Once the claim process fails, authors may be stuck. The author could not proceed and had no alternative except contacting Goodreads Support.

- Posting personal information in public forums may be unsafe. A librarian warned the author not to post her email address publicly.

- Identity corrections may depend entirely on Goodreads staff. Librarians have no authority to resolve author-claim issues, leaving authors dependent on support response times.

This incident possibly demonstrates how Goodreads' identity-matching system can misassign books to incorrect author profiles and how new authors may struggle to claim their pages due to form errors or system limitations. It also possibly shows the strict boundary between librarian permissions and staff-only functions, leaving authors with limited options when automated systems fail.

Context and Overview

This chapter documents a publicly visible discussion in the Goodreads Librarians Group in March 2026. An author named Alex reported that his book *The Rules of the Dance: Men Being Too Intimate* had been assigned to the wrong author profile — another writer with the same first and last name. Although a librarian attempted to correct the issue, the book remained linked to the incorrect profile.

The author noted that this was not the first time this had happened and expressed frustration with repeatedly needing to request corrections. This incident possibly illustrates how Goodreads' name-matching system can repeatedly misassign works when multiple authors share the same name, and how manual corrections may not persist. The transcript is preserved exactly as it appeared.

Snapshot Transcript (Verbatim)

Goodreads Librarians Group discussion *Book & Author Page Issues > Book linked to wrong author of same name 7 views Comments Showing 1–4 of 4 Date Range: March 2–6, 2026*

message 1: by Alex (new) *Mar 02, 2026 04:34AM "The Rules of the Dance: Men Being Too Intimate* (ASIN B0GQQ6RC8L) The book is currently listed under wrong author with the same name as me. Correct link should be connected to goodreads.com/byalexo Thank you, Alex"

message 2: by Scott (new) *Mar 02, 2026 06:34AM* "That one wasn't on your profile, but I found another one that was. Done."

message 3: by Alex (new) *Mar 04, 2026 06:33AM* "HI Scott, thanks, but *THE RULES OF THE DANCE* is under wrong author page linked to Alex O, who has *The Kidnapping of Mr. and Mrs. T for Thanksgiving Dinner* currently. It should be under goodreads.com/byalexo with other 9 titles (inc. *The Time We Had*). Same Name author is confusing and I hate to do this every time. Sorry for all the trouble."

message 4: by Alex (new) *Mar 06, 2026 06:02AM "The Rules of the Dance: Men Being Too Intimate* Just checking in, if any librarians can help on this!"

Analysis and Interpretation

- Same-name authors may be frequently conflated. Goodreads appears to rely heavily on name matching rather than authoritative metadata, causing books by different authors with identical names to be merged or misassigned.

- Manual corrections may not apply to the intended edition. The librarian moved a different book but did not correct the one the author reported, suggesting that the system may not clearly distinguish between multiple works with similar metadata.

- Authors may need to request corrections repeatedly. The author stated that this happens "every time," indicating a recurring pattern of misattribution.

- Identity collisions may persist even when authors have established profiles. The author's correct profile already contained nine titles, yet the new book was still assigned to a different "Alex O."

- Librarian intervention alone may not resolve systemic issues. The thread ended without resolution, and the author's follow-up received no response.

- Misattribution may affect discoverability and catalog integrity. When books are assigned to the wrong author, readers may not find the correct works, and authors lose control over their public bibliography.

This incident possibly demonstrates how Goodreads' reliance on name-based identity matching can repeatedly misassign works when multiple authors share the same name. It also possibly shows how manual corrections may be incomplete or misapplied, leaving authors to request fixes repeatedly. The pattern aligns with other chapters in this book: identity instability, repeated misattribution, and limited author control over their catalog presence.

Context and Overview

This chapter documents a publicly visible discussion in the Goodreads Librarians Group that began in November 2024 and resurfaced in March 2026. In 2024, an author named C.W. attempted to claim his novel *Children of the Fog*, which had been incorrectly attributed to a deceased children's author with the same initials. A librarian created a new author page, instructed him to claim it, and marked the request as complete.

Nearly two years later, in March 2026, the author returned to report that the misattribution had reappeared: clicking the author hyperlink on his book once again led to the wrong author profile. Although the book was attached to his claimed profile, the system continued to redirect to the incorrect author page. A librarian manually corrected the name again and instructed the author not to change it.

This incident possibly illustrates how Goodreads' automated ingestion and identity-matching systems may override or revert manual corrections, even long after a librarian has marked an issue as resolved. It also possibly shows how authors may believe their identity is stable only to discover that the system has silently undone the fix. The transcript is preserved exactly as it appeared.

Snapshot Transcript (Verbatim)

Goodreads Librarians Group discussion *Book & Author Page Issues > DONE: Unable to claim my novel due to incorrect author attribution 3 views Comments Showing 1–6 of 6 Date Range: November 21, 2024 – March 5, 2026*

message 1: by C.W. (new) *Nov 21, 2024 06:51AM* "Hi, I am hoping someone can help me claim my novel. It is currently attributed to a deceased children's author rather than myself. Here is my horror novel *Children of the Fog* (ISBN: 9781963733013): https://www.goodreads.com/book/show/2... Here is the incorrect author attribution: https://www.goodreads.com/author/show... Here is my

Goodreads account I just created:
https://www.goodreads.com/user/show/1... I am unsure how to claim my book since it is already attributed to the author CW Anderson. Please help / let me know what steps I need to take? Thank you so much! Best, Chris"

message 2: by Shim (new) *Nov 21, 2024 08:01AM (last edited Nov 21, 2024 08:02AM)* "Here is your new author page:
https://www.goodreads.com/author/show... Please click the link at the bottom where it says 'Is this you?' to claim the page and Goodreads will connect it to your account. This request is complete. Please edit the title / subject of your post and add [done] so other Librarians know it is complete. For future reference your author page has the name as 'C.W.^^^^Anderson' where '^' represents a space. If you add any books in the future, if you set the author field like that they will automatically show up correctly."

message 3: by C.W. (new) *Nov 22, 2024 06:28AM* "Thank you so much Shim!"

message 4: by C.W. (new) *Mar 04, 2026 06:09AM* "Hi, Thanks again for your help back in 2024! I just discovered that if you click on the author hyperlink for my book, it still takes you to the incorrect C.W. Anderson. I claimed this book as mine and it is attached to my profile, so not sure what else to do. Please let me know? Thank you! Chris"

message 5: by Scott (new) *Mar 04, 2026 07:15AM* "I have corrected the name. Don't change it again."

message 6: by C.W. (new) *Mar 05, 2026 08:19PM* "I see it corrected now. Thank you so much!"

Analysis and Interpretation

- Manual corrections may not persist long term. The misattribution reappeared nearly two years after the librarian marked the issue "done," suggesting that automated processes may override or revert manual fixes.

- Claiming an author page may not guarantee stability. The author successfully claimed his page in 2024, yet the system still linked his book to the wrong author in 2026.

- Goodreads' ingestion pipeline may reassign books based on name matching. The reversion suggests that external metadata feeds or automated matching rules continue to treat "C.W. Anderson" as a single identity.

- Authors may be unaware that their catalog has changed. The author discovered the reversion only by clicking the hyperlink years later, indicating that Goodreads does not notify authors when identity changes occur.

- Librarians may be able to correct the issue manually but cannot prevent future reversion. The librarian's instruction — "Don't change it again" — implies that the system may revert if the author adjusts metadata or if automated ingestion runs again.

- Identity collisions may persist across years. The same misattribution that occurred in 2024 resurfaced in 2026, demonstrating long-term instability for authors with shared names.

This incident possibly demonstrates how Goodreads' identity-matching system may undo corrections long after they are made, leaving authors with unstable catalog entries even after following all recommended steps. It also possibly shows how automated ingestion and name-based matching can override librarian actions, contributing to identity instability, repeated misattribution, and the fragility of manual corrections in a system driven by automated metadata ingestion.

Context and Overview

This chapter documents a publicly visible discussion in the Goodreads Librarians Group from February to March 2026. An author named Alex reported that his book *The Night We Found What We Lost: Men Being Too Intimate* had been assigned to the wrong author profile — another writer with the same name. A librarian corrected the issue on February 16 and marked the request as "Done."

However, by March 2, the author discovered that the book had been moved back to the wrong profile. The librarian confirmed that she had moved it correctly the first time but that "someone removed it" afterward. She then moved it again and noted that if it was removed again, it was not her doing.

This incident possibly illustrates how Goodreads' author-identity system, or processes operating within it, may undo or override corrections even after a librarian has completed a request. It also possibly shows how identity collisions between authors with the same name can create ongoing instability, requiring repeated manual intervention. The transcript is preserved exactly as it appeared.

Snapshot Transcript (Verbatim)

Goodreads Librarians Group discussion *Book & Author Page Issues > (DONE) Book linked to wrong author of same name 9 views Comments Showing 1–6 of 6 Date Range: February 16 – March 4, 2026*

message 1: by Alex (new) *Feb 16, 2026 05:15PM "The Night We Found What We Lost: Men Being Too Intimate* The book is currently listed under wrong author with the same name as me. Correct link should be connected to goodreads.com/byalexo Thank you, Alex"

message 2: by Tami (new) *Feb 16, 2026 06:11PM* "Done."

message 3: by Alex (new) *Feb 16, 2026 06:37PM* "Thanks Tami!"

message 4: by Alex (new) *Mar 02, 2026 06:52AM* "Noticed it wasn't moved to correct author page. Correct author placement should be goodreads.com/byalexo. Currently having 8 books. The wrong author (same name as me) is the one who wrote *2:19 AM: a book of poetry*."

message 5: by Tami (new) *Mar 02, 2026 08:56AM (last edited Mar 02, 2026 09:40AM)* "Yes, I moved it on February 16th but someone removed it from your profile. I put it back again, please check: https://www.goodreads.com/book/show/2... If it gets removed again, it wasn't me."

message 6: by Alex (new) *Mar 04, 2026 06:28AM* "Thanks"

Analysis and Interpretation

- Corrections marked "Done" may not persist. The book was moved correctly on February 16 but reverted to the wrong profile by March 2.

- Identity collisions between authors with the same name may cause recurring errors. Goodreads' name-matching system repeatedly assigned Alex's books to another "Alex O" who writes unrelated works.

- Manual corrections may be undone by automated processes or other users. The librarian stated that "someone removed it," indicating that corrections are not locked or protected.

- Authors may need to monitor their own catalog for silent reversions. The author discovered the reversion only by checking his profile weeks later.

- Librarians may be able to fix the issue but cannot prevent future overrides. The librarian's warning — "If it gets removed again, it wasn't me" — suggests that the system or other actors may continue to reassign the book.

- The system may not notify authors when changes occur. The author received no alert that his book had been moved back to the wrong profile.

This incident possibly demonstrates how Goodreads' identity-matching system, or processes operating within it, may override or undo corrections even after a librarian has marked an issue as resolved. It also possibly shows how authors with common names may face ongoing instability, requiring repeated manual intervention to maintain accurate attribution.

Context and Overview

This chapter documents a publicly visible discussion in the Goodreads Librarians Group from November 2025 through March 2026. An author named K.B. Lee repeatedly reported that each new book in her *Wicked Riffs* series was being automatically assigned to a different author with the same name. Despite librarians correcting the issue each time, the problem recurred with every new release.

The librarians explained that Goodreads differentiates authors with identical names by inserting invisible spacing into the name field (for example, "K.B.^^Lee"). However, because the books were being auto-imported from external sources, the system consistently defaulted to the other K.B. Lee profile. This created a recurring cycle in which each new book required manual intervention to move it to the correct author page.

This incident possibly illustrates how Goodreads' name-matching system may fail to reliably distinguish between authors with identical names, how auto-imported books may bypass or override manual corrections, and how authors may be forced into an ongoing loop of requesting fixes. The transcript is preserved exactly as it appeared.

Snapshot Transcript (Verbatim)

Goodreads Librarians Group discussion *Book & Author Page Issues >* *[DONE] Can't claim my book it is with another author with same name 20 views Comments Showing 1–16 of 16 Date Range: November 12, 2025 – March 2, 2026*

message 1: by K.B. (new) *Nov 12, 2025 10:24AM* "I would appreciate it if you would remove *Born to Rock Wicked Riffs Book* from the K.B. Lee it is under, and add it to my K.B. Lee Author Page: https://www.goodreads.com/author/show..."

message 2: by Astrid (new) *Nov 12, 2025 12:12PM* "Your name is differentiated to others with the same name by an extra space. This means that your name will be added like: K.B.^^Lee. I've added the extra space, so it should be on your page now."

message 3: by K.B. (new) *Nov 12, 2025 12:45PM* "Thank you."

message 4: by Astrid (new) *Nov 12, 2025 01:30PM* "You're welcome! Let us know if you need help with anything else."

message 5: by K.B. (new) *Dec 09, 2025 09:59PM* "The same thing happened with the second book in the series. *Shooting Stars Wicked Riffs Book 2* was posted to the same K.B. Lee you removed Book 1 from."

message 6: by Scott (new) *Dec 10, 2025 06:29AM* "Done. Include link in future."

message 7: by K.B. (new) *Dec 10, 2025 09:22AM* "I will. Thank you so much!!"

message 8: by K.B. (new) *Dec 23, 2025 08:02PM (last edited Dec 23, 2025 08:03PM)* "I hate to have to ask you for help, but it has happened again. My book, *Rock On Wicked Riffs Book 3*, is listed under the same wrong K.B. Lee. I'm publishing monthly and have 4 more books in this series. I fear this will happen each time."

message 9: by Shim (new) *Dec 23, 2025 08:09PM (last edited Dec 23, 2025 08:10PM)* "Moved. Yes, if the books are auto-imported they will land on the default profile each time."

message 10: by K.B. (new) *Dec 24, 2025 03:34PM* "Thank you!"

message 11: by K.B. (new) *Jan 26, 2026 08:15PM* "*Tangled Notes Wicked Riffs Book 4* is listed under the same wrong K.B. Lee. Please move Tangled Notes to my author page."

message 12: by Astrid (new) *Jan 27, 2026 04:50PM* "Done! I've added it to your series as well."

message 13: by K.B. (new) *Jan 27, 2026 07:54PM* "Thank you!!"

message 14: by K.B. (new) *Feb 23, 2026 05:34PM* "*Love Song Wicked Riffs Book 5* is listed under the same wrong K.B. Lee. Please move Love Song to my author page."

message 15: by K.B. (new) *Mar 02, 2026 10:47AM* "[Bump]"

message 16: by Scott (new) *Mar 02, 2026 10:52AM* "done"

Analysis and Interpretation

- Auto-import may override manual corrections. Each new book in the series was automatically assigned to the other K.B. Lee, regardless of previous fixes.

- Invisible spacing may be used as a workaround for same-name authors. Goodreads differentiates authors with identical names by inserting hidden spaces (for example, "K.B.^^Lee"), a fragile method that depends on precise metadata formatting.

- Authors with common names may face recurring misattribution. The author noted that she expected this to happen every month — and it did.

- Manual intervention may be required for every new release. Librarians had to move each book individually, month after month.

- The system may default to the "first" or "original" profile. As one librarian explained, auto-imported books will land on the default profile each time.

- Authors may need to monitor their catalog continuously. She discovered each misattribution only after publication, requiring repeated correction requests.

- Librarians may be able to fix individual cases but cannot change the underlying behavior. The root cause — Goodreads' name-matching and auto-import logic — remains unaddressed.

This incident possibly demonstrates — through repeated librarian admissions — that Goodreads' identity-matching and auto-import systems may create a persistent misattribution loop for authors with identical names. It also possibly shows how manual corrections cannot prevent future misassignments, requiring authors to remain in an ongoing cycle of monitoring and requesting fixes.

Context and Overview

This chapter documents a publicly visible discussion in the Goodreads Librarians Group on March 2, 2026. An author named Thomas Gloom discovered that someone else had created an author profile using his name and had already claimed his forthcoming book *Stories With Horror & Heart (Volume 4)*. He was unable to claim the book or attach it to his real account.

Librarians explained that Goodreads differentiates authors with identical names by inserting invisible spaces into the name field (for example, "Thomas^^Gloom"). They advised him to notify librarians whenever he publishes a new book so they can manually "disambiguate" it. When he asked whether he could change the spacing in his name, he was told to contact Goodreads Support — and warned that switching to the default profile would likely cause his books to be repeatedly misassigned.

This incident possibly illustrates how Goodreads' identity-matching system may allow another person to claim an author's book simply by sharing the same name, how fragile the spacing-based workaround can be, and how authors may be required to rely on manual disambiguation for each new release. The transcript is preserved exactly as it appeared.

Snapshot Transcript (Verbatim)

Goodreads Librarians Group discussion *Book & Author Page Issues > Someone Else Has Claimed My Book 9 views Comments Showing 1–7 of 7 Date: March 2, 2026*

message 1: by Thomas (new) *Mar 02, 2026 09:19AM* "As the title suggests, someone else has created a profile with my author name (Thomas Gloom) and claimed my pre-order book *Stories With Horror & Heart (Volume 4)*. I'd like to get this book claimed on my actual account, but can't figure out how."

message 2: by Dee (new) *Mar 02, 2026 09:21AM* "Can you post the GR book link in this thread — someone will disambiguate it and get it added to your profile."

message 3: by Thomas (new) *Mar 02, 2026 09:23AM* https://www.goodreads.com/book/show/2...

message 4: by Dee (new) *Mar 02, 2026 09:25AM* "Edited — for reference — your profile in the GR database is Thomas^^Gloom (2 spaces between first and last). Whenever you write a new book or have a new one imported — let ppl know, so they can easily disambiguate."

message 5: by Thomas (new) *Mar 02, 2026 09:32AM* "Oh my! Is there a way I can change that, or am I stuck with the 2 spaces?"

message 6: by Scott (new) *Mar 02, 2026 09:35AM* "You can ask support if they will swap you with the default profile."

message 7: by Dee (new) *Mar 02, 2026 09:41AM* "But just know that if you switch to the default — you'll end up with books not yours when they are ported over — personally, I'd recommend keeping yours as is."

Analysis and Interpretation

- Someone else may be able to claim a book simply by sharing the same name. The author's pre-order title was already attached to a different "Thomas Gloom" profile created by another user.

- Goodreads may use invisible spacing to differentiate authors. The author's correct profile was stored as "Thomas^^Gloom," a workaround that is invisible to readers and fragile in practice.

- Authors may need to notify librarians every time they publish. Librarians instructed the author to alert them for each new book so they could manually "disambiguate" it.

- Switching to the default profile may create new risks. Librarians warned that moving to the default "Thomas Gloom" profile would likely cause unrelated books to be repeatedly assigned to him.

- Identity collisions may be treated as normal and expected. The librarians' responses assumed that same-name conflicts would continue indefinitely.

- Authors may be unable to fix their own identity formatting. The author asked whether he could change the spacing in his name; he was told only Goodreads Support could do that.

- The system may provide no protection against impersonation or accidental claiming. Goodreads allowed another user to create a profile with the same name and claim the book without verification.

This incident possibly demonstrates how Goodreads' identity-matching system may allow misattribution and even accidental "claiming" of an author's work by someone else with the same name. It also possibly shows how fragile the platform's disambiguation system can be, relying on invisible spacing and manual intervention rather than stable identifiers. The pattern aligns with other chapters in this book: identity instability, misattribution, and the need for constant manual correction.

Context and Overview

This chapter documents a publicly visible discussion in the Goodreads Librarians Group on February 27–28, 2026. I reported that multiple newly released titles from my own imprint, Two Worlds Universe Press, were once again assigned to the wrong author profile. Despite prior corrections and a consistent publisher of record, Goodreads continued to route new releases to another author with the same name.

Librarians attempted to correct the entries manually, but the books reverted again. The librarian explained that my metadata had been altered — specifically, the invisible spacing Goodreads uses to differentiate authors with identical names — and noted that Kindle editions must remain labeled as Kindle editions because Amazon's ingestion pipeline enforces that format. When Kindle editions did not match the imprint designation on the ISBNs I assigned, the system defaulted to Amazon's interpretation rather than my publisher metadata.

This incident possibly illustrates how Goodreads' ingestion system may override publisher-controlled metadata, how fragile the spacing-based identity system can be, and how corrections may be undone within hours. The transcript is preserved exactly as it appeared, with only the removed line omitted.

Snapshot Transcript (Verbatim)

Goodreads Librarians Group discussion *Book & Author Page Issues > wrong author yet again (edit) 24 views Comments Showing 1–8 of 8 Date Range: February 27–28, 2026*

message 1: by James *Feb 27, 2026 08:27PM* "my books yet again are under the wrong author. i assumed this would have been a simple add for goodreads as my current work and the new ones are under the same imprint. if there is a way to ensure works from my imprint are imported correctly, please do so 'Two Worlds Universe Press'. please lock that author from receiving my works or do what needs to be done to fix this. i have more releasing and i don't want to keep doing this. the books that have been attributed to another author are:

https://www.goodreads.com/book/show/2...
https://www.goodreads.com/book/show/2...
https://www.goodreads.com/book/show/2...
https://www.goodreads.com/book/show/2...
https://www.goodreads.com/book/show/2...
https://www.goodreads.com/book/show/2...”

message 2: by YellowBlackKing *(last edited Feb 27, 2026 11:00PM) Feb 27, 2026 10:56PM* “Hi, I'm sorry, your links aren't working for me. I've moved to your page what I found from searching, feel free to tell me the ISBN of any more missing. To generally solve this issue, you can ask the Goodreads support if they could make you the default profile. Please note books from other authors with your name might be automatically imported onto there then though. You could also try to manually create all your (physical or non-Kindle) books before the Amazon bot does so.”

message 3: by James *Feb 28, 2026 04:23AM* “there is just one more for the upcoming releases with isbns that has not been switched. this will cover this year's releases. Divine Wrath. https://www.goodreads.com/book/show/2...”

message 4: by YellowBlackKing *Feb 28, 2026 11:51AM* “Done :)”

message 5: by James *Feb 28, 2026 01:33PM* “somehow it got reconnected to the same author again.”

message 6: by YellowBlackKing *(last edited Feb 28, 2026 02:00PM) Feb 28, 2026 01:52PM* “You have removed the extra spaces from the author field, those separate you from the default profile. Also, please stop changing the format of your Kindle editions to ebook, this has to be sent to the Goodreads support now for them to deal with it.”

message 7: by James *(last edited Feb 28, 2026 04:08PM) Feb 28, 2026 03:42PM* “i didn't assign an isbn for just kindle editions. they are releasing elsewhere as well. so would not a simple ebook be more accurate as that is what the assignment is in bowker. As the publisher of record i would appreciate this going up to support. i should get to correct errors that are being forced into my metadata. i choose the release date set in bowker. i can legally decide which date to release in various outlets. i am correcting the data to match my bowker metadata."

message 8: by YellowBlackKing *Feb 28, 2026 09:52PM* "Kindle editions get automatically imported from Amazon & should stay as Kindle editions. As Goodreads is owned by Amazon, this is the site standard."

Analysis and Interpretation

- Imprint consistency may not prevent misattribution. Even though all titles were published under Two Worlds Universe Press, Goodreads continued assigning them to the wrong author.

- Invisible spacing may determine identity. Goodreads differentiates same-name authors using hidden spaces, and if those spaces are altered — even unintentionally — the system may reassign the book to the default profile.

- Corrections may be undone within hours. A book moved to the correct profile in the morning was reassigned to the wrong author by afternoon.

- Amazon ingestion may override publisher metadata. Kindle editions must remain labeled as Kindle editions because Amazon's pipeline enforces that format, regardless of Bowker metadata.

- Authors may be unable to control their own metadata. Attempts to correct format and release-date metadata to match Bowker were rejected by Goodreads.

- Librarians may be unable to lock profiles or prevent future misassignments. The librarian suggested contacting Goodreads Support, acknowledging that the problem cannot be solved at the librarian level.

- Manual creation may be suggested as a workaround. The librarian recommended creating all editions manually before Amazon's bot imports them — a burden placed entirely on the author.

This incident possibly demonstrates how Goodreads' ingestion system may override my publisher-of-record metadata, undo corrections, and repeatedly misassign works even when the author and imprint are consistent. It also possibly shows how fragile the identity system can be and how little control I may have over my own catalog.

Context and Overview

This chapter documents a publicly visible discussion in the Goodreads Librarians Group spanning December 2024 through February 2026. Multiple authors attempted to remove books from their author pages — either because they had delisted the work, no longer wanted it associated with them, or because the book had been misattributed to them due to same-name collisions.

Goodreads librarians explained that published books cannot be deleted from the database, even if the author has withdrawn them from sale. They also clarified that librarians cannot modify claimed author pages, and that only Goodreads Support can separate name variants or move books off an author's profile. The thread ends with two additional authors reporting misattributed books on February 28, 2026.

This incident possibly illustrates Goodreads' rigid policy against removing published works, the limitations of librarian permissions, and the ongoing problem of same-name misattribution. The transcript is preserved exactly as it appeared.

Snapshot Transcript (Verbatim)

Goodreads Librarians Group discussion *Book & Author Page Issues > Remove book from author page 35 views Comments Showing 1–7 of 7 Date Range: December 19, 2024 – February 28, 2026*

message 1: by Daniel (new) *Dec 19, 2024 10:54AM* "Is it possible to delete this book? I'm the author, I've de-listed this everywhere and I'd like to have it removed from here as well."

message 2: by Scott (new) *Dec 19, 2024 10:58AM* "No, we don't delete published books. It would interfere with users' reading histories, and prevent them from logging them in the future. Goodreads is not a store."

message 3: by Daniel (new) *Dec 19, 2024 11:07AM* "That's fair. Can it be removed from my author page?"

message 4: by Scott (new) *Dec 19, 2024 11:30AM* "In this case it may be possible, but you'd have to talk to support as librarians cannot work with claimed author pages. Since your other books are just under Daniel Frost, you can have that be your profile, and the book with the D.F. can be elsewhere. Tell support that you'd like to separate the name variants, but hold onto Daniel Frost as your claimed profile. They should be able to do it."

message 5: by Scott (new) *Dec 23, 2024 10:32AM* "Looks like support did the opposite of what should have been done. No surprise there. Anyway, the book appears to be gone."

message 6: by Tina (new) *Feb 28, 2026 06:01PM* "This book about IBS was not written by me. Please remove it from my page. Thanks! https://www.goodreads.com/book/show/2..."

message 7: by Courtney (new) *Feb 28, 2026 06:54PM* "My book is listed under someone else of the same name and I would like it moved to my profile. It's titled *Stolen Bases* (ISBN: 979-8249605445). Thank you!"

Analysis and Interpretation

- Published books may not be deleted, even at the author's request. Goodreads treats its database as a permanent bibliographic record rather than a storefront, so delisted or withdrawn works remain visible.

- Authors may be unable to remove books from their own pages. Once an author page is claimed, librarians lose the ability to detach or relocate books, leaving authors without direct control.

- Only Goodreads Support may separate name variants or correct misattribution. Librarians repeatedly directed authors to Support for identity-related issues, emphasizing that they cannot resolve these conflicts themselves.

- Support actions may be incorrect or contradictory. In Daniel's case, Support "did the opposite of what should have been done," according to the librarian, showing that even official interventions may introduce new errors.

- Same-name collisions may continue to cause misattribution. Both Tina and Courtney reported books appearing on their pages that they did not write, underscoring the persistence of name-based identity conflicts.

- Authors may need to rely on manual intervention for identity corrections. Goodreads provides no automated mechanism to prevent or resolve same-name conflicts, requiring repeated human fixes.

- The system may treat author identity as mutable and unstable. Books can be moved, misassigned, or removed from profiles based on internal processes authors cannot see or control.

This incident possibly demonstrates how Goodreads' policies and system limitations may leave authors with little control over their own bibliographic identity. Even when authors delist a book, adjust their catalog, or encounter misattribution, they must rely on Support — and Support may act unpredictably. The pattern aligns with other chapters in this book: identity instability, misattribution, and the fragility of corrections within Goodreads' ingestion system.

Context and Overview

This chapter documents a publicly visible discussion in the Goodreads Librarians Group from January to February 2026. A first-time author, Ajeet Pratap, discovered that his debut novel *Arsenal of The Gods* had been automatically assigned to another author with the same name because his author page did not yet exist when the book was added to Goodreads.

A librarian moved the book to a blank profile and instructed him to claim it. The author followed the procedure, but his author-program request remained unprocessed for more than a month. He returned asking for help because he needed author-page approval to run giveaways and promotional events. The librarian explained that Goodreads librarians cannot assist with author-program approvals and directed him to Goodreads Support.

This incident possibly illustrates how Goodreads' author-claim system may stall indefinitely, how librarians have no authority to approve or escalate claims, and how new authors may be left unable to promote their work due to system delays. The transcript is preserved exactly as it appeared.

Snapshot Transcript (Verbatim)

Goodreads Librarians Group discussion *Book & Author Page Issues > Incorrect author 'Arsenal of The Gods' 7 views Comments Showing 1–5 of 5 Date Range: January 27 – February 28, 2026*

message 1: by Ajeet Pratap (new) *Jan 27, 2026 03:16AM* "As this book is my first book and my Author page was not ready when this book was added on Goodreads, my book *Arsenal of The Gods* was attached to another author of same name. Kindly add this book in my profile. My profile also needs to be changed to Author profile. Book Name: *Arsenal of The Gods* Publisher: Om Books International ISBN 10 – 9363952231 ISBN 13 – 78-9363952232" message 2: by YellowBlackKing (new) *Jan 29, 2026 12:25AM* "I've moved this to a blank profile. You can read here how to claim it."

message 3: by Ajeet Pratap (new) *Jan 29, 2026 07:55PM* "Thank you so much for your quick response. I have claimed the book as per the suggested procedure."

message 4: by Ajeet Pratap (new) *Feb 28, 2026 02:33AM* "Hi, I claimed the book as per the procedure but the request has not been processed or approved yet. Kindly process it as soon as possible as I need to conduct giveaways and other events to promote the book. If my profile needs to be changed to 'author' profile, kindly do that too. Please pardon me for pushing but my book needs more visibility."

message 5: by YellowBlackKing (new) *Feb 28, 2026 11:48AM (last edited)* "I'm sorry but I cannot help you with this problem since librarians aren't affiliated with the Goodreads company. Please contact support."

Analysis and Interpretation

- New authors may be especially vulnerable to misattribution. Because the author page did not exist when the book was added, Goodreads assigned the debut novel to another author with the same name.

- Librarians may be able to move books but cannot approve author claims. The librarian created a blank profile and moved the book, but could not convert that profile into an approved author page.

- Author-program requests may remain unprocessed for long periods. The author waited more than a month without any update from Goodreads Support.

- Authors may be unable to run giveaways or promotions without an approved author page. Goodreads' promotional tools remain locked until the author-program request is approved.

- Librarians may repeatedly redirect authors to Support for identity-level issues. This reflects a structural separation between catalog maintenance (librarians) and identity control (Goodreads staff).

- The system may provide no visibility into claim status. The author had no way to know whether his request was pending, rejected, or lost.

This incident possibly demonstrates how Goodreads' author-claim system may leave new authors in limbo, unable to control their own identity or promote their work. It also reinforces the broader pattern documented throughout this book: misattribution may be common, corrections may be fragile, and authors may need to rely on a slow and opaque support process for identity-related issues.

Context and Overview

This chapter documents a publicly visible discussion in the Goodreads Librarians Group from February 12–27, 2026. An author publishing under the name V. N. Alexander discovered that her novel *The Girlie Playhouse* had been misattributed to the well-known romance author Victoria Alexander. Although librarians were able to move the book to the correct profile, the author attempted to update her author-page name to avoid future confusion.

Goodreads declined the request. Because earlier books had been published under "Victoria," the system would not allow her to change her author-page name to her current publishing identity. The librarian recommended consolidating all works under the older name, even though the author had intentionally adopted a new pen name to prevent misattribution.

This incident possibly reinforces the systemic challenges created by Goodreads' rigid name-locking policy, its limited ability to accommodate author rebranding, and the structural bias toward preserving older metadata even when it contributes to ongoing confusion.

Snapshot Transcript (Verbatim)

Goodreads Librarians Group discussion *Book & Author Page Issues > My novel is attributed to the wrong author 10 views Comments Showing 1–5 of 5 Date Range: February 12–27, 2026*

message 1: by V. (new) *Feb 12, 2026 03:48PM* "My novel, *The Girlie Playhouse* is misattributed to the author 'Victoria Alexander.' https://www.goodreads.com/book/show/2... This is my author page https://www.goodreads.com/author/show... I am publishing under 'V. N. Alexander' now to avoid confusion with the romance author 'Victoria Alexander.'"

message 2: by Chantel (new) *Feb 13, 2026 05:57AM* "Hello, your links are just directing me to general pages instead of specific author pages. I found your book, however, and it seems to be attributed to 'V. N Alexander'. https://www.goodreads.com/book/show/2... Please check your link and share a direct link to your author page so we can verify that this is correct."

message 3: by V. (new) *Feb 26, 2026 03:50PM* "Yes, V. N. Alexander is my name. I am also known as Victoria N. Alexander This is my profile: https://www.goodreads.com/author/show... I would prefer to change my profile to V. N. Alexander, if that's allowed."

message 4: by Scott (new) *Feb 26, 2026 04:21PM* "You can't change your name because books have been published under Victoria. The most economical thing to do is simply have everything under that profile, so I have moved the book."

message 5: by V. (new) *Feb 27, 2026 10:05AM* "Thank you Scott"

Analysis and Interpretation

- Misattribution to a more famous author may be common. Goodreads initially assigned *The Girlie Playhouse* to the well-known romance author "Victoria Alexander," despite the book belonging to a different writer.

- Goodreads may lock author names once books exist under them. Because earlier works were published under "Victoria," the author was prohibited from updating her profile to her current pen name "V. N. Alexander."

- The system may prioritize legacy metadata over current author identity. Even when the author intentionally rebranded to avoid confusion, Goodreads required all works to remain under the older name.

- Librarians may be able to move books but cannot change author-page names. Identity-level changes require Goodreads Support, and the policy governing those changes is restrictive.

- Authors may have limited control over their own catalog identity. The author's attempt to prevent future misattribution was denied, leaving her vulnerable to continued confusion with the more famous author.

- The recommended solution may be consolidation, not correction. The librarian advised keeping everything under the older name, even though that name actively contributed to misattribution.

This incident possibly demonstrates how Goodreads' rigid name-locking policy may prevent authors from managing their own identities, even when existing metadata creates ongoing confusion. It reinforces the broader pattern documented throughout this book: Goodreads' systems may be designed to preserve older data rather than protect authors from misattribution or identity collisions.

Context and Overview

This chapter documents a publicly visible discussion in the Goodreads Librarians Group on February 26, 2026. An author, Dale E. Lehman, reported that his novel *Penitence* had not been linked to his author page. He noted that this was not the first time this had happened and suspected that Goodreads was mishandling his middle initial during ingestion.

A librarian investigated and discovered that Goodreads had assigned the book to a different "Dale E. Lehman" who held the default profile. The librarian asked the author to confirm which works belonged to him and which belonged to the other writer. After clarification, the librarian moved the correct books to the correct profile.

This incident possibly illustrates how Goodreads' ingestion system may struggle with authors who share identical names, how middle initials may not reliably prevent collisions, and how authors may need to monitor their catalog repeatedly for misattribution.

Snapshot Transcript (Verbatim)

Goodreads Librarians Group discussion *Book & Author Page Issues > "Penitence" not linked to my author page 8 views Comments Showing 1–5 of 5 Date: February 26, 2026*

message 1: by Dale (new) *Feb 26, 2026 08:35AM* "*Penitence* didn't get linked to my author page Dale E. Lehman. FYI, I'm catching up on several missing books. This has happened before. I think it's an issue with how my middle initial comes across, but I'm not sure. Thank you."

message 2: by Scott (new) *Feb 26, 2026 09:12AM* "Apparently there is another Dale E. Lehman who has the default profile. Are any other of these books yours? https://www.goodreads.com/author/show..."

message 3: by Dale (new) *Feb 26, 2026 11:14AM (last edited)* "'Writers in Lockdown' and the 'Indies Unlimited' collections are anthologies that I have stories in. I believe they are showing on my profile. There is another

Dale E. Lehman who authored the telecommunications and practical spreadsheets books. Those are not mine."

message 4: by Scott (new) *Feb 26, 2026 11:17AM* "Ok, I have moved them."

message 5: by Dale (new) *Feb 26, 2026 11:34AM* "Thank you!"

Analysis and Interpretation

- Middle initials may not prevent identity collisions. Even though the author published as "Dale E. Lehman," Goodreads still assigned his book to another writer with the exact same name.

- Goodreads may maintain a "default profile" for each name. The librarian identified that the other Dale E. Lehman held the default profile, causing new books to be routed there automatically.

- Authors may need to manually verify which works belong to them. The librarian asked the author to confirm which books were his and which belonged to the other writer, indicating that Goodreads cannot reliably distinguish between them.

- Anthology contributions may complicate attribution. The author's short stories in anthologies were correctly linked, but standalone works were misassigned, showing inconsistent handling across formats.

- Librarians may be able to move books but cannot prevent future misattribution. The fix is manual and temporary; nothing in the system prevents the next book from being assigned to the wrong profile again.

- The author may experience this repeatedly. He explicitly stated, "This has happened before," reinforcing the pattern of ongoing instability.

This incident possibly demonstrates how Goodreads' ingestion system may struggle with authors who share identical names, even when middle initials are present. It also possibly shows how authors may need to monitor their catalog repeatedly and rely on manual corrections, as the system provides no automated safeguards against same-name collisions.

Context and Overview

This chapter documents a publicly visible discussion in the Goodreads Librarians Group on February 24–25, 2026. A new author, Chad Martin, discovered that Goodreads had automatically assigned forty-five books — none of which he wrote — to his author page. He had published only a single Bible study book, yet Goodreads had merged him with dozens of unrelated authors who shared his name.

Librarians explained that the issue occurred because Goodreads had placed him on the default profile for the name "Chad Martin," a profile that already contained books dating back to 2021. They also described Goodreads' internal method of differentiating authors with identical names: invisible spacing inserted between first and last names. Support intervened and moved him to a new profile, but the correction was handled "in a different way than normal," and the librarian noted that Goodreads Support often performs these fixes inconsistently.

This incident possibly illustrates how Goodreads' identity-matching system may overwhelm a new author with dozens of misattributed works, how fragile the spacing-based disambiguation system can be, and how even librarians may express uncertainty about Goodreads' internal processes.

Snapshot Transcript (Verbatim)

Goodreads Librarians Group discussion *Book & Author Page Issues > Books assigned to me that aren't mine 9 views Comments Showing 1–7 of 7 Date Range: February 24–25, 2026*

message 1: by Chad (new) *Feb 24, 2026 05:08AM* "This is Chad Martin. I wrote a Bible class/small group study book titled, *From Eve to Abram Following God's Promise—A Study of Genesis 1–11*. This is the only book I have written. Goodreads has assigned 45 books to me from other authors named Chad Martin. How can these be removed? My page should only have the one book I have written, which is in paperback and kindle. Thank you."

message 2: by Liralen (new) *Feb 24, 2026 07:44AM* "Please contact Support: https://www.goodreads.com/about/contact Include a link to the book you wrote, and they will move you and your book to a new profile."

message 3: by Chad (new) *Feb 24, 2026 12:07PM* "https://www.goodreads.com/book/show/2... It's in paperback and Kindle: or on Amazon: https://www.amazon.com/Eve-Abram-Foll..."

message 4: by Scott (new) *Feb 24, 2026 12:09PM* "Again, please contact support."

message 5: by Tawnya (new) *(last edited Feb 25, 2026 09:38AM) Feb 25, 2026 01:31AM* "What they are not explicitly explaining is that no one assigned those books to you. They were there first, the oldest is from 2021. 20 hours ago, YOU were assigned a profile that was already taken, the default one. I have contacted support and asked that YOU be moved. I told them which editions were yours. I do not understand why they are still assigning the default profiles to common names. I thought they had stopped."

message 6: by Tawnya (new) *(last edited Feb 25, 2026 04:04AM) Feb 25, 2026 03:58AM* "OK, support handled it in a different way than normal. Usually, they have the author keep the one space (default) and add spaces to the name. Then the books that do not belong to the author are moved to a new default. Be thankful there were only 45 books. Dan Brown had over 1000 that were not his. Most were for a comic book artist. The man himself (at that time) had only written 7 books. I spent over half the year cleaning up that mess. I wish they would handle more profile requests this way. It is more logical to move the new person and their books to a new profile instead of having to schlep a ton of books out the original one. If it hasn't been explained to you, Goodreads differentiates authors by adding spaces between the first and last name. You now have two spaces. That is how your profile should have been set up from the beginning. Readers do not see the difference. It is an internal sorting procedure. The other books still have your visage attached to them, but that will go away soon. Give it 48 hours. As I said before, support usually moves authors another way. I had to go into the default and remove all of your information."

message 7: by Chad (new) *Feb 25, 2026 06:49AM* "Tawnya wrote: 'OK, support handled it in a different way than normal. Usually, they have the author keep the one space (default) and add spaces to the name. Then the books that do not belong to the author are…'"

Analysis and Interpretation

- Default profiles may cause mass misattribution. Goodreads assigned the new author to a pre-existing "Chad Martin" profile containing forty-five unrelated books.

- Same-name collisions may be treated as normal. Librarians explained that the books "were there first," meaning the system simply merged the new author into an existing identity.

- Goodreads may use invisible spacing to differentiate authors. The author's corrected profile now contains two hidden spaces between first and last name — a workaround invisible to readers but critical to the system.

- Support may handle identity corrections inconsistently. The librarian noted that Support "handled it in a different way than normal," and expressed confusion about Goodreads' internal logic.

- Librarians may need to manually remove the author's information from the default profile. This indicates that Goodreads does not automatically clean up misassigned data.

- Misattributed books may continue to display the author's photo temporarily. The librarian warned that the author's image would remain attached for up to forty-eight hours.

- The scale of misattribution may be enormous. The librarian referenced a previous case where "Dan Brown" had more than one thousand misassigned books.

This incident possibly demonstrates how Goodreads' identity system may overwhelm new authors with dozens of misattributed works, how fragile the spacing-based disambiguation system can be, and how even librarians may express frustration with Goodreads' internal processes. It reinforces the broader pattern documented throughout this book: identity instability, misattribution, and inconsistent corrections.

Context and overview

This chapter documents a Goodreads Librarians Group thread from February 24–25, 2026. Author Iryna Burda reported that two completely different books had been incorrectly merged as editions of the same work. Both carried similar or identical titles in Russian, but they were distinct titles with different ASINs and different content. One is a book of fables ("Пчела и бабочка"), and the other is the first volume in a separate series.

The librarian initially declined to separate them, citing the shared title and noting that librarians cannot edit ASINs and that only the author can set the primary edition. Iryna clarified that the books had been merged earlier by mistake and asked for the works to be separated so she could manage them herself, including recreating the Kindle edition if necessary.

This incident possibly illustrates how Goodreads' work–edition model may collapse distinct titles into a single record, how difficult it can be for authors to reverse an incorrect merge, and how ASIN control is constrained by system limitations. The transcript is preserved exactly as it appeared.

Snapshot transcript (verbatim)

Goodreads Librarians Group discussion *Book & Author Page Issues > Please separate different books and update ASIN (Author: Iryna Burda) 5 views Comments Showing 1–4 of 4 Date Range: February 24–25, 2026*

message 1: by Iryna (new) *Feb 24, 2026 12:00PM* "Hello! I am a Goodreads Author (Iryna Burda). There is an error in the catalog: two different books have been incorrectly combined as editions of the same work. Please SEPARATE these two books. They are different titles, not editions of the same book. The book 'Пчела и бабочка' should have ASIN: B0FHJMGZ53. Please update it and set this edition as Primary. The other book (Book 1 in the series) has ASIN: B0FB64S2BM. It should be a separate standalone work/series entry. Please fix the ASIN link so my Kindle readers can find the correct book. Thank you!"

message 2: by Scott (new) *Feb 24, 2026 12:07PM* "They have the same title though. We cannot edit ASINs, and only the author can set the primary edition."

message 3: by Iryna (new) *Feb 25, 2026 03:45AM* "Thank you for your reply. However, there is a misunderstanding. These are NOT the same book. 'Пчела и бабочка' is a book of fables, and the other one (ASIN: B0FB64S2BM) is a different book entirely. They were incorrectly merged by a librarian earlier. Please SEPARATE them first. Once they are separate works, I will be able to manage them. Regarding the ASIN: The current record has the wrong ASIN. Since I am the author, if you cannot change it, please DELETE the incorrect Kindle edition, and I will manually create a new one with the correct ASIN (B0FHJMGZ53). Please help me separate these two different titles so they don't sit on the same page."

message 4: by Iryna (new) *Feb 25, 2026 03:47AM* "Iryna wrote: 'Thank you for your reply. However, there is a misunderstanding. These are NOT the same book. "Пчела и бабочка" is a book of fables, and the other one (ASIN: B0FB64S2BM) is a different book entirel…'"

Analysis and interpretation

- Incorrect work merge may collapse distinct books into a single record. Two unrelated titles were treated as mere "editions" of one work because they shared a title, erasing their separate identities.

- Librarian limitations may prevent timely correction. The librarian initially refused to separate the books based on title similarity and noted that librarians cannot edit ASINs, shifting responsibility back to the author.

- The author may be trapped by a prior librarian error. Iryna explained that a librarian had previously merged the books incorrectly; she could not reverse the merge herself and had to request that it be undone.

- ASIN rigidity may force destructive workarounds. Goodreads would not adjust the incorrect ASIN, leaving the author to request deletion of the Kindle edition and recreate it from scratch to restore accurate metadata.

- Discoverability may be harmed until the works are separated. Kindle readers were directed to the wrong book, undermining both sales and reader trust.

This incident possibly reinforces a broader pattern: once Goodreads' systems or librarians collapse distinct works into a single record, authors may face structural resistance and limited tools to restore accurate identity and metadata. With the post unresolved at the time of this snapshot, the author remained harmed by the issue.

This chapter documents a publicly visible discussion in the Goodreads Librarians Group on February 24–25, 2026. Author Lee Nash reported that her entire list of authored books—built over years—had disappeared from her profile. She could see only her shelves and favorite books, not the works she had written or contributed to.

Librarians discovered that she was no longer listed on her own books and that her identity had split into two separate profiles: a user profile she controlled and a separate author profile containing her books, which she had not created. A past change to her last name, switching it to all caps, may have triggered Goodreads to strip her author status and revert her to a standard user profile. Goodreads Support restored only two of her books after she contacted them, leaving the rest missing. The librarians instructed her to claim the author profile, reapply for Goodreads Author status, and manually link each book one by one.

This incident possibly illustrates how fragile Goodreads' author-identity system can be, how easily an author may lose access to their own catalog, and how difficult it is to restore a collapsed author profile once the system has split or overwritten it. The transcript is preserved exactly as it appeared.

Snapshot Transcript (Verbatim)

Goodreads Librarians Group discussion *Book & Author Page Issues > My books list has disappeared 11 views Comments Showing 1–9 of 9 Date Range: February 24–25, 2026*

message 1: by Lee (new) *Feb 24, 2026 12:00PM* "Dear Librarians, Help! My book list, which I have painstakingly added to over the years, with your kind assistance, is not visible any more. Is this redeemable, or should I start from scratch? Thank you, Lee Nash"

message 2: by Scott (new) *(last edited Feb 24, 2026 12:12PM) Feb 24, 2026 12:03PM* "Do you mean books that you have written? Some links would be helpful. If you are talking about your personal book activity, that has nothing to do with librarians, and you should contact support."

message 3: by Lee (new) *(last edited Feb 24, 2026 12:11PM) Feb 24, 2026 12:09PM* "Yes, I mean books that I have written and books to which I have contributed, eg: https://www.goodreads.com/book/show/5... Please could you add a link here to direct me to the right group. Previously the librarians added my books to my profile."

message 4: by Scott (new) *Feb 24, 2026 12:13PM* "I don't see that you were ever on that book record, but I have added your name. I guess you'll just have to link to each book and we can add you."

message 5: by Lee (new) *(last edited Feb 24, 2026 01:23PM) Feb 24, 2026 12:32PM* "Thanks. Just to be clear, I would like to reinstate my book list, LEE NASH'S BOOKS on my profile: https://www.goodreads.com/user/show/4... At the moment, I see only my favourite books and my bookshelves. NB I see my books on a profile with the same name, but I did not create it... https://www.goodreads.com/author/show... I flagged this issue on Nov 19, 2022. All the books are here but they need to be added to my profile. https://www.goodreads.com/author/list... With these exceptions (I guess it's the same book). This has nothing to do with me: https://www.goodreads.com/book/show/4... https://www.goodreads.com/book/show/5..."

message 6: by Scott (new) *Feb 24, 2026 12:37PM* "If all the books on that list are yours, claim the profile. Currently you only have a user profile. You need to go through an application process to become a GR Author."

message 7: by Emily (new) *(last edited Feb 24, 2026 12:39PM) Feb 24, 2026 12:38PM* "At some point you changed your last name to all caps, which may have caused all of the books to go off your profile. I'm not sure. When that happens your profile goes back to a user profile. I would contact Support and ask them to help you claim this profile again. You will need to re-copy and paste your link to the profile. https://www.goodreads.com/about/contact"

message 8: by Lee (new) *(last edited Feb 24, 2026 01:17PM) Feb 24, 2026 12:46PM* "OK thanks for your help! I'll contact Support."

message 9: by Lee (new) *Feb 25, 2026 02:02AM* "Hi Scott and Emily, I now have my own author page:

https://www.goodreads.com/author/list... I sent the entire list of books to Support but only two are listed. Here are the others, please could you add them? https://www.goodreads.com/book/show/4...
https://www.goodreads.com/book/show/4...
https://www.goodreads.com/book/show/3...
https://www.goodreads.com/book/show/2...
https://www.goodreads.com/book/show/1...
https://www.goodreads.com/book/show/5...
https://www.goodreads.com/book/show/6...
https://www.goodreads.com/book/show/3...
https://www.goodreads.com/book/show/4...
https://www.goodreads.com/book/show/5...
https://www.goodreads.com/book/show/5...
https://www.goodreads.com/book/show/5...
https://www.goodreads.com/book/show/3...
https://www.goodreads.com/book/show/3...
https://www.goodreads.com/book/show/6...
https://www.goodreads.com/book/show/5...
https://www.goodreads.com/book/show/5...
https://www.goodreads.com/book/show/2...
https://www.goodreads.com/book/show/1...
https://www.goodreads.com/book/show/2... This page still exists. I assumed it would be deleted or merged with my author page. https://www.goodreads.com/author/show... Perhaps the system takes time to catch up...? Please advise. Thank you. Lee Nash"

Analysis and Interpretation

- Author identity may silently collapse. Lee's author status disappeared without warning, reverting her to a user profile and detaching her entire catalog.

- Goodreads may create duplicate author identities without the author's knowledge. A second "Lee Nash" author page existed, containing her books, even though she had never created it.

- A simple metadata change may break the author profile. Changing her surname to all caps appears to have triggered Goodreads to treat her as a new identity and strip her author status.

- Support may restore only partial data. After she contacted Goodreads Support, only two books were returned to her profile; the rest required manual librarian intervention.

- Authors may need to manually relink every book. The librarian instructed her to provide links to each title individually, indicating that Goodreads offers no automated recovery.

- Duplicate author pages may remain active indefinitely. The older author page persisted even after she claimed a new one, leaving her identity split across profiles.

- Identity instability may persist for years. Lee first reported the issue in 2022, and it resurfaced in 2026, showing long-term fragility in Goodreads' identity system.

This incident possibly demonstrates how Goodreads' identity system may fracture an author's presence, erase their catalog, and create duplicate profiles that require extensive manual repair. It reinforces the broader pattern documented throughout this book: Goodreads' author-identity infrastructure may be fragile, easily disrupted, and slow to correct.

Context and Overview

This chapter documents a publicly visible discussion in the Goodreads Librarians Group on February 24, 2026. An author, T. Lamar Taylor, discovered that his book *The Gloom: Arachnophobia* had been linked to a dummy author profile ("T. Taylor"). When he attempted to correct the author name inside the book's metadata, Goodreads automatically removed the book from his account and created a duplicate author profile.

He also found that Goodreads had generated three separate versions of his book, each treated as a separate edition rather than a unified work record. A librarian restored the book to his profile and submitted a request to Goodreads Support to update his author-page name. The librarian also warned him not to edit the author field again, because Goodreads interprets such edits as a signal to detach the book from the author entirely.

This incident possibly illustrates how Goodreads may interpret author-field edits as identity changes, how easily duplicate author profiles can be created, and how fragile the work–edition structure becomes when multiple versions of a book exist. The transcript is preserved exactly as it appeared.

Snapshot Transcript (Verbatim)

Goodreads Librarians Group discussion *Book & Author Page Issues > My book isn't under my profile 9 views Comments Showing 1–4 of 4 Date: February 24, 2026*

message 1: by T. (new) *Feb 24, 2026 09:28AM* "Hello, I am the author of *The Gloom: Arachnophobia.* My book was linked to a dummy author profile named T. Taylor. After going into the book details to change the author name to T. Lamar Taylor, the book was removed from my account. The book still shows T. Lamar Taylor as the author but it isn't under my account. It seems to have created a duplicate account. Also, there seems to be three separate versions of my book for each Edition.

Can they all be merged into one entity? Book page: https://www.goodreads.com/book/show/2... All 3 versions of book: https://www.goodreads.com/author/show... Author page: https://www.goodreads.com/author/dash... Please help. Thank you."

message 2: by T. (new) *Feb 24, 2026 09:29AM* "also, it seems T. Taylor the name given to this author profile I'm using. can someone help me change it to T. Lamar Taylor?"

message 3: by T. (new) *Feb 24, 2026 09:48AM* "thank you"

message 4: by Shim (new) *(last edited Feb 24, 2026 10:49AM) Feb 24, 2026 10:49AM* "Books moved back to your profile. I sent a request to Goodreads Support to update your page name to match the book covers. Don't edit the author field on your books as that removes it from your profile."

Analysis and Interpretation

- Editing the author field may detach the book from the author. Goodreads interprets changes to the author field as a signal that the book belongs to a different person, causing it to be removed from the author's profile.

- Dummy profiles may be created automatically. The book was initially assigned to "T. Taylor," a placeholder identity generated by Goodreads' ingestion system.

- Correcting the author name may create a duplicate profile. When the author changed the name to "T. Lamar Taylor," Goodreads created a new author identity rather than linking the book to his existing account.

- Multiple editions may be treated as separate works. Goodreads generated three separate entries for the same book instead of merging them into a unified work record.

- Librarians may be able to move books but cannot change author names. The librarian had to escalate the name-change request to Goodreads Support.

- The system may penalize authors for correcting metadata. The librarian explicitly warned: "Don't edit the author field on your books as that removes it from your profile."

- Identity instability may be built into the system. A simple metadata correction triggered a cascade of unintended consequences: book removal, duplicate profiles, and fragmented editions.

This incident possibly reinforces a recurring pattern throughout this book: Goodreads' identity system may be brittle, easily confused by metadata edits, and prone to creating duplicate profiles and fragmented work records. Authors attempting to correct errors may inadvertently trigger new ones.

Context and Overview

This chapter documents a publicly visible discussion in the Goodreads Librarians Group from February 17–23, 2026. A debut author, Neel, attempted to claim his book *The Corridor of Strugglers*, which had been automatically assigned to the wrong author due to a name match. He provided proof of authorship, including his publisher page and ISBN, and asked librarians to move the book to his profile.

Librarians informed him that he could only claim the other author profile, not the user profile he actually controlled. When he attempted to join the Goodreads Author Program, his claim was rejected twice. Goodreads Support then told him that he could not be recognized as the author unless he had either a KDP account or an author website verified by Amazon. Because he had neither, Goodreads refused to link his book to his account.

This incident possibly illustrates how Goodreads' author-verification system may depend on Amazon-linked identity, preventing legitimate authors from claiming their own books unless they participate in Amazon's ecosystem. The transcript is preserved exactly as it appeared.

Snapshot Transcript (Verbatim)

Goodreads Librarians Group discussion *Book & Author Page Issues > Claim a book I wrote 11 views Comments Showing 1–6 of 6 Date Range: February 17–23, 2026*

message 1: by Neel (new) *Feb 17, 2026 04:36AM* "Hi Librarians, I'm the author of *The Corridor Of Strugglers* listed here: https://www.goodreads.com/book/show/2... It is currently attached to the wrong author profile due to a name match. Here's proof of authorship: Publisher page: https://notionpress.com/author/1461122 ISBN: 979-8902966944 Currently linked to: https://www.goodreads.com/author/show... Should be linked to: https://www.goodreads.com/user/show/1... Could you please move the book to my author profile (or advise on the next steps)? Thank you so much!"

message 2: by YellowBlackKing (new) *Feb 17, 2026 05:20AM* "You currently have an user profile but you can claim this one: https://www.goodreads.com/author/show..."

message 3: by Neel (new) *Feb 19, 2026 08:55AM* "Thank you for your response. However, it's twice now that I've tried to claim the book to my account and join the author program, and it failed both times. I'm a new author and it is my debut book. Any type of assistance would be greatly appreciated. Cheers."

message 4: by Scott (new) *Feb 19, 2026 08:57AM* "Contact support. https://www.goodreads.com/about/contact"

message 5: by Neel (new) *Feb 23, 2026 10:17AM* "I tried. They said I either need an author website referring my contacts or a KDP account, and since I have neither of those, they can't link the book to my account."

message 6: by YellowBlackKing (new) *Feb 23, 2026 12:59PM* "I'm sorry but we cannot help you with this problem since librarians aren't affiliated with the Goodreads company /:"

Analysis and Interpretation

- Goodreads may require Amazon-linked identity to verify authorship. Support refused to recognize the author without either a KDP account or an Amazon-verified website, even though he provided independent proof.

- Goodreads may not function as an independent catalog. The requirement for Amazon-based verification shows that Goodreads' author-program identity checks are tied directly to Amazon's infrastructure rather than to bibliographic evidence.

- Legitimate authors may be blocked from claiming their own books. Despite providing ISBNs, publisher links, and proof of authorship, the author was denied the ability to claim his work.

- Librarians may have no authority over author-program verification. They repeatedly directed him to Support, acknowledging that they cannot override Amazon-based requirements.

- The system may force authors into Amazon's ecosystem. Without KDP or an Amazon-verified website, authors cannot control their own identity on Goodreads, even when misattribution is clear.

- Name-match misattribution may remain uncorrectable without author-program approval. The book stayed attached to the wrong author because the author could not pass Amazon-based verification.

This incident possibly reinforces a critical pattern documented throughout this book: Goodreads' identity system may be fragile and structurally dependent on Amazon's verification mechanisms. Authors outside the Amazon ecosystem may face barriers to correcting misattribution, claiming their own books, or establishing an author presence.

This project did not begin as an investigation. It began as a simple study. I wanted to understand whether the problems affecting my own imprint—misassigned books, incorrect author links, and unstable metadata—were normal. I assumed they were. I expected to find a handful of isolated cases, the kind of routine catalog noise that occurs on any large platform.

What emerged instead was a pattern.

Across dozens of publicly visible threads, spanning years and involving authors from many backgrounds, the same issues appeared repeatedly: collapsed author profiles, merged works, duplicate identities, incorrect ASINs, stalled author claims, and metadata that reverted or changed without the author's consent. My own experience was not an outlier. It appeared to be part of a broader set of behaviors described consistently by authors and librarians.

This book grew out of that realization. It is no longer the small, neutral study I intended to write. It is a record of what authors reported during this period, drawn entirely from publicly visible discussions in the Goodreads Librarians Group. It documents what authors said they encountered, what librarians attempted within the limits of their tools, and what the system appeared to allow or prevent. It reflects the constraints of Amazon-linked verification, the limits of volunteer authority, and the fragility of the identity structures that determine where a book appears and under whose name.

This book is not a legal guide, and it does not offer legal advice. It does not claim to describe Goodreads' internal systems, intentions, or proprietary mechanisms. It reflects only what was visible in the public record at the time: authors describing their experiences, librarians explaining their capabilities and limitations, and the outcomes that followed.

The incidents collected here show how easily an author's catalog can be disrupted: books assigned to the wrong person, duplicate author profiles created without warning, merged works that collapse distinct titles, vanished book lists, stalled author claims, and metadata that changes or reverts without the author's input. None of these cases are hypothetical. They are the lived experiences of authors trying to maintain accurate identities and correct metadata within a system that, based on these reports, often behaved unpredictably.

Goodreads is not a neutral archive. It is a dynamic, user-editable platform owned by Amazon, shaped by automated ingestion, volunteer librarian actions, and support-team policies. Its identity system—built on name matching, invisible spacing, and automated profile creation—was not designed to scale cleanly across millions of books and thousands of overlapping author names. The result, as reflected in these discussions, is a system where errors may occur easily, corrections may be undone, and authors may lose access to their own catalog without warning.

The librarians who appear in these threads are volunteers. They cannot change ASINs, cannot override Amazon-based verification requirements, cannot approve author status, and cannot prevent the system from creating default profiles. Their role is limited to catalog maintenance, not identity governance, and they repeatedly stated that they must follow Amazon's guidelines and rules. The issues documented here appear structural rather than personal.

This book does not attempt to diagnose the internal causes of these problems or predict how the platform may evolve. It reflects a specific moment in time. Goodreads has existed since 2007, and the thread from which these examples were drawn spans nearly two decades of reported issues. The cases in this book represent only a small fraction of that history; at the time this snapshot was taken, the thread contained more than 146,000 discussions.

What this record provides is clarity. It shows how authors may lose control of their catalog identity, how metadata may be overridden or misrouted, how duplicate profiles may appear, how merged works may collapse distinct titles, and how corrections may trigger new problems. It shows the limits of librarian authority, the dependency on Amazon-linked verification, and the fragility of the systems that attempt to differentiate authors with identical names.

For new authors, this information is not meant to discourage. It is meant to prepare. Publishing does not end when a book is released. It continues in the metadata, in the catalog, and in the identity systems that determine where a book appears and under whose name. When those systems behave unpredictably, the impact is real: misattributed books, fragmented author identities, lost discoverability, and confusion for readers.

This book is a snapshot of that reality.

— Section Two: Key Terms and Their Real-World Impact on Authors

The threads collected in this book rely on a set of recurring terms—*misattribution, default profiles, merged works, edition fragmentation, author claims, ASIN mismatches,* and others. These are not abstract concepts. They are the mechanisms through which authors either maintain control of their catalog identity or lose it. Understanding these terms is essential for any new author entering the publishing ecosystem, because each one represents a point where the system can fail, and where vigilance becomes necessary.

This section defines these terms in clear, accessible language and explains how they affect authors in practical, real-world ways. These definitions are not legal, technical, or exhaustive. They are descriptive, based on the patterns visible in the public discussions documented in this book. They reflect how these terms functioned during the snapshot period covered here.

Misattribution

Misattribution occurs when a book is assigned to the wrong author. This can happen because two authors share the same name, because metadata was incomplete or inconsistent, or because Goodreads' ingestion system matched a new book to an existing profile based on name alone.

Impact on authors:

- Readers searching for the correct author may never find the book.

- Reviews, ratings, and visibility accumulate under the wrong person.

- A debut author may be buried under dozens of unrelated titles.

- Promotional efforts become ineffective because the book is not linked to the author's page.

- The author may be unable to claim the book or correct the error without passing Goodreads' verification requirements.

Misattribution is one of the most common and most damaging issues documented in this book.

Default Profiles

A default profile is the first author profile created for a given name. Goodreads automatically routes new books to this profile unless metadata explicitly differentiates them.

Impact on authors:

- New authors with common names are often merged into an existing identity.

- Books published years apart by unrelated people appear under one profile.

- Authors may inherit dozens or even hundreds of books they did not write.

- Correcting the issue requires manual intervention from librarians or support.

- Even after correction, future books may still be misrouted.

Default profiles are a structural feature of Goodreads, not an error. But their existence creates ongoing instability for authors with non-unique names.

Invisible Spacing (Internal Name Differentiation)

Goodreads differentiates authors with identical names by inserting invisible spaces between the first and last name. Readers cannot see these spaces, but the system relies on them.

Impact on authors:

- A single missing or altered space can collapse two identities into one.
- Editing the author field can remove the spacing and trigger misattribution.
- Authors may unknowingly break their own profiles by correcting metadata.
- Librarians must manually adjust spacing to restore identity separation.
- The system provides no visible indicator that spacing is being used.

This mechanism is fragile and easily disrupted, yet it underpins the entire identity-matching system.

Merged Works

Merged works occur when Goodreads treats two different books as editions of the same title. This often happens when titles are similar or identical, even if the content is unrelated.

Impact on authors:

- Distinct books lose their individuality and appear as one.
- Readers may purchase or review the wrong book.
- The author cannot set the correct primary edition.
- ASINs and ISBNs may be mismatched, breaking Kindle links.
- Series structure becomes incoherent or misleading.

Merged works are difficult to reverse and often require librarian intervention.

Edition Fragmentation

Edition fragmentation occurs when Goodreads creates multiple separate entries for what should be a single work. This can happen when metadata differs slightly across formats or platforms.

Impact on authors:

- Reviews and ratings are split across multiple pages.
- Readers may not see all available formats.
- The book's visibility is diluted.
- The author must request merges to consolidate the editions.
- Fragmentation can recur if metadata is inconsistent.

Fragmentation is the opposite of a merged work, but both problems reduce discoverability.

Author Claims and the Goodreads Author Program

To control their author page, authors must join the Goodreads Author Program. This requires verification, which during this snapshot often depended on Amazon-linked identity.

Impact on authors:

- Without approval, authors cannot edit their own profiles.
- They cannot run giveaways or use promotional tools.
- They cannot correct misattribution or update metadata.
- Claims may be rejected if the author lacks a KDP account or an Amazon-verified website.
- Support responses vary, and claims may stall for weeks or months.

The author-program gatekeeping documented in these threads directly affects an author's ability to maintain a stable presence on the platform.

ASIN and ISBN Mismatches

ASINs (Amazon identifiers) and ISBNs (international book identifiers) must match the correct edition. Goodreads often imports ASINs automatically from Amazon.

Impact on authors:

- Incorrect ASINs break Kindle links.
- Readers may be directed to the wrong book.
- Authors cannot edit ASINs themselves.
- Incorrect Kindle editions may need to be deleted and recreated.
- Mismatches can cause merged works or edition fragmentation.

ASIN errors disproportionately affect authors who rely on Kindle visibility.

Duplicate Author Profiles

Duplicate profiles occur when Goodreads creates multiple identities for the same author, often due to metadata inconsistencies or author-field edits.

Impact on authors:

- Books may be split across multiple profiles.
- Readers may follow the wrong profile.
- Reviews and ratings become scattered.
- The author must request merges, which may take time.
- Duplicate profiles may persist even after correction.

Identity fragmentation is one of the most persistent issues documented in this book.

Vanished Book Lists and Lost Author Status

In some cases, authors reported that their entire list of authored books disappeared from their profile, often due to name changes or system resets.

Impact on authors:

- Years of catalog building can vanish instantly.

- The author may revert to a user profile.

- Books must be relinked manually, one by one.

- Duplicate profiles may appear during the process.

- Support may restore only part of the list.

This is one of the most disruptive failures an author can experience on the platform.

Why These Issues Matter

These terms are not technical jargon. They represent real obstacles that directly affect an author's ability to reach readers. When a book is misattributed, merged, fragmented, or lost, the consequences are immediate:

- Readers cannot find the correct book.

- Reviews accumulate under the wrong profile.

- Promotional efforts fail.

- Search visibility collapses.

- Sales and readership suffer.

- The author's professional identity becomes unstable.

For new authors—especially those without a large platform—these issues can determine whether a book reaches its audience at all.

— Section Three: How These Problems Affect Discoverability and an Author's Ability to Reach Readers

The issues documented throughout this book—misattribution, merged works, duplicate profiles, failed author claims, ASIN mismatches, vanished book lists, and identity fragmentation—are not merely technical inconveniences. They have direct, measurable consequences for authors, especially new ones. Publishing is not only the act of writing a book; it is the act of ensuring that book can be *found, recognized,* and *correctly attributed* in the systems readers use to discover new titles. Goodreads is one of the largest of those systems. When its internal mechanisms fail, the effects ripple outward into visibility, credibility, and the author's ability to build an audience.

This section explains how these problems impact authors in real-world terms, why they matter, and why vigilance is necessary even though no universal remedy exists.

Discoverability: The First and Most Fragile Link

Discoverability is the foundation of an author's career. A book that cannot be found cannot be read, reviewed, recommended, or purchased. Goodreads is a major discovery platform, used by millions of readers to track books, explore genres, follow authors, and browse recommendations. When a book is misattributed or fragmented across multiple entries, its discoverability collapses.

How misattribution harms discoverability

When a book is assigned to the wrong author:

- It disappears from the correct author's page.

- Readers searching for the author will not see it.

- The book becomes buried under unrelated titles.

- Search results may prioritize the wrong author, especially if that author is more established.

- The book may accumulate reviews and ratings under someone else's profile, distorting both authors' reputations.

For a debut author, this can be catastrophic. A first book often determines whether a second book finds an audience. If the first book is invisible, the author's career may stall before it begins.

How merged works harm discoverability

When two different books are merged into one work record:

- Readers cannot distinguish between them.

- Reviews for one book appear under another.

- The author cannot set the correct primary edition.

- The book may be miscategorized or mis-shelved.

- Series order becomes incoherent.

Readers rely on accurate metadata to decide what to read. When that metadata is wrong, they may skip the book entirely.

How edition fragmentation harms discoverability

When a book appears in multiple separate entries:

- Reviews and ratings are split across pages.

- The book appears less popular than it is.

- Readers may not see all available formats.

- The algorithm may not recommend the book because engagement is diluted.

Fragmentation weakens the book's presence in the ecosystem.

Credibility: The Author's Public Identity

An author's profile is not just a list of books; it is a public identity. It signals legitimacy, professionalism, and continuity. When that identity fractures, credibility suffers.

Duplicate profiles undermine credibility

When Goodreads creates multiple author profiles for the same person:

- Readers may follow the wrong profile.

- Books may be scattered across pages.

- The author appears inconsistent or inactive.

- Engagement metrics become fragmented.

- The author loses control over how they are presented.

Readers expect a single, coherent author identity. When the system fails to provide one, the author appears less established.

Vanished book lists erase history

When an author's entire list of works disappears:

- Years of catalog building are lost.
- The author may appear to have no published works.
- Past contributions (anthologies, collaborations, translations) vanish.
- The author must rebuild their presence manually, often title by title.
- Duplicate profiles may appear during the process, further confusing readers.

This is not a minor inconvenience. It is a collapse of the author's public record.

Failed author claims block professional tools

Without author-program approval:

- Authors cannot update their own profiles.
- They cannot run giveaways or promotions.
- They cannot correct misattribution.
- They cannot add missing editions.
- They cannot communicate with followers.

When Goodreads requires Amazon-linked identity (KDP or an Amazon-verified website), authors outside that ecosystem face barriers that have nothing to do with the legitimacy of their work.

Sales and Reader Engagement: The Downstream Effects

Goodreads does not sell books, but it influences sales. Readers use it to decide what to buy, what to borrow, and what to recommend. When metadata is wrong, the downstream effects are significant.

Broken ASINs break Kindle visibility

When a Kindle edition has the wrong ASIN:

- The "Buy on Amazon" link may lead to the wrong book.

- Readers may be unable to find the correct edition.
- Sales may be diverted to another author.
- The author may need to delete and recreate the Kindle edition.
- Reviews may accumulate under the wrong ASIN.

For authors who rely on Kindle sales, this is a direct financial impact.

Misattribution affects algorithms

Goodreads' recommendation engine relies on:

- Ratings
- Reviews
- Shelves
- Reader engagement
- Author follows

When these signals are misrouted:

- The book is not recommended to the right audience.
- The author's visibility drops.
- The book may never reach the readers who would enjoy it.

Algorithms amplify accuracy. They also amplify errors.

Series continuity breaks

When books in a series are misassigned, merged, or fragmented:

- Readers cannot follow the correct reading order.
- Series pages become incoherent.
- Engagement drops because readers cannot navigate the sequence.
- The author loses the momentum that series fiction normally provides.

Series readers are loyal, but only when the system supports them.

Career Momentum: The Long-Term Impact

For many authors, especially new ones, the first few years of publishing determine whether they continue. When metadata errors accumulate:

- The author may appear less active than they are.
- Their catalog may look smaller or inconsistent.
- Their books may be overshadowed by unrelated works.
- Their promotional efforts may fail because the book is not linked correctly.
- They may lose opportunities for reviews, interviews, or collaborations.
- They may struggle to build a readership.

These are not theoretical harms. They are practical, measurable obstacles that affect real careers.

Why Vigilance Is Necessary

This book does not offer remedies because there are no universal solutions. The system is large, complex, and shaped by automated ingestion, volunteer librarians, and Amazon-linked verification. Authors must:

- Monitor their profiles regularly.
- Check new editions for accuracy.
- Verify that books appear under the correct identity.
- Contact support when necessary.
- Keep records of their metadata.
- Understand that corrections may take time.
- Accept that some issues may recur.

This is not a failure of authors. It is a reality of the current ecosystem.

— Section Four: Context, Continuity, and the Value of Documentation

The threads collected in this book represent only a fraction of the experiences authors have shared over the years, but they are part of a much larger continuum. The Goodreads Librarians Group thread from which these examples were drawn has existed for nearly nineteen years. Over that time, thousands of authors have posted questions, reported errors, asked for corrections, and sought help navigating a system that is both vast and fragile. The issues documented here are not new, and they are not isolated. They are part of a long, ongoing pattern shaped by the scale of the platform, the limitations of its tools, and the complexity of global publishing metadata.

This book captures a snapshot of that pattern—nothing more, nothing less. It does not claim to represent every experience, every problem, or every solution. It does not attempt to diagnose the internal workings of Goodreads or Amazon beyond what librarians themselves openly stated in these threads, nor does it speculate about future changes. It simply records what authors encountered during this period, how librarians responded, and how the system behaved. It is a moment in time, preserved so that new authors can understand the landscape they are entering.

Goodreads is one of the largest online communities for readers and authors. Its influence is significant, but its infrastructure is not infallible. The platform was built in 2007, acquired by Amazon in 2013, and has grown far beyond its original scale. Millions of books, authors, and readers interact within a system that must reconcile data from publishers, distributors, retailers, libraries, users, and automated ingestion pipelines. Errors are inevitable and often baked in. What matters is not whether the system is perfect—it is not—but how authors can navigate it with awareness and realistic expectations.

The cases documented in this book show a consistent pattern of challenges that authors may face. Books can be assigned to the wrong author. Author profiles can split, duplicate, or disappear. Works can be merged incorrectly or fragmented across multiple entries. Author claims can stall or be denied. Metadata can be overwritten by ingestion or user edits. Visibility can be reduced by algorithmic misrouting. Identity can be tied to Amazon-linked verification requirements that authors cannot control. These are not isolated incidents. They are recurring behaviors within a system that was never designed to scale cleanly across millions of overlapping identities.

This book does not offer universal remedies because there are none. Each author's situation is shaped by their name, their metadata, their publisher, their distribution channels, and the timing of ingestion. What resolves quickly for one author may persist for months for another. Some regain control of their profiles; others remain stuck in verification loops. The only consistent theme is the need for awareness.

Awareness does not mean fear. It means understanding how the system behaves. It means checking your author page periodically, verifying that new editions appear correctly, monitoring for duplicate profiles or merged works, and keeping metadata consistent across platforms when possible. It means contacting support when necessary, even if responses vary. Goodreads is not a static archive but a living system shaped by user edits, automated ingestion, and Amazon-linked identity rules.

For new authors, this awareness is part of the publishing process. Writing the book is only the beginning. Publishing requires attention to metadata, distribution, catalog accuracy, and platform identity. Goodreads is one of the places where those elements converge. When the system works, it helps readers discover new books and follow authors. When it fails, it can obscure a book, fragment an author's identity, or misdirect readers entirely.

This book exists to illuminate those failures—not to condemn them, but to document them. Transparency is valuable. Awareness is valuable. Knowing what can go wrong helps authors prepare for what may happen. Knowing the limits of the system helps authors set realistic expectations. Knowing the history of the thread—nearly two decades of authors reporting similar issues—helps authors understand that these problems are not personal, not unique, and not a reflection of their professionalism.

This is not a guide, a manual, or a set of instructions. It is a record. A snapshot. A reflection of how things stood during this period.

Platforms evolve. Policies change. Systems are updated. The issues documented here may be resolved in the future, or they may persist. This book does not predict or prescribe. It simply shows what authors experienced and how the system responded.

The value of documentation is clarity. When authors understand the landscape, they can navigate it more effectively. When they know what to watch for, they can act sooner. When they know that others have faced similar challenges, they can approach the process with patience rather than confusion or frustration. Awareness does not eliminate obstacles, but it reduces the shock of encountering them.

This closing chapter marks the end of the snapshot, but not the end of the story. The Goodreads Librarians Group thread continues. Authors continue to publish. Metadata continues to flow. Systems continue to evolve. The challenges documented here will change, but the need for awareness will remain. Publishing is not only about creativity. It is about stewardship—of your work, your identity, and your presence in the systems readers use to find you.

This book is offered in that spirit: not as instruction, not as advice, but as illumination. A record of what authors faced. A reminder that they are not alone. And a testament to the importance of understanding the systems that shape how books reach the world.

Final Note from the Author

Thinking back on the events that led me to this project, I can only share a few reflections with other authors. These are not legal instructions or professional guidance—just the perspective of someone who has been through the process.

It has helped me to secure official copyright registration through the agency available in my country. Understanding the rights that copyright provides has been grounding, especially when navigating situations where metadata or attribution did not behave as expected. Every country handles these matters differently, and each author's circumstances will vary, but learning the basics of your own rights can make a difference.

When something feels wrong—whether on Goodreads or anywhere else—it can be important to understand how to assert the rights you already have. In my experience, those rights can sometimes feel overlooked or minimized, and each author has to find their own way of responding to that. Diligence and persistence have carried me through more than once, and they may help others as well.

Writing means different things to different people. For some, it is a business; for others, a hobby; for others still, something deeply personal. Whatever it is for you, I hope you continue. I hope the words come when you need them, and that new worlds open up as you create them.

Public source links used in this work

Goodreads Librarians Group – Book removal request http: //www.goodreads.com/topic/show/24369650-book-removal-request

Goodreads Librarians Group – Book attributed to wrong author http: //www.goodreads.com/topic/show/24366583-book-attributed-to-wrong-author

Goodreads Librarians Group – Books attributed to another author http: //www.goodreads.com/topic/show/24367009-books-attributed-to-another-author

Goodreads Librarians Group – Book attributed to wrong author [done] http: //www.goodreads.com/topic/show/24365806-book-attributed-to-wrong-author-done

Goodreads Librarians Group – Description Errors: Enshittification http: //www.goodreads.com/topic/show/23778394-incomplete-since-january-description-errors-enshittification

Goodreads Librarians Group – Four invalid editions http: //www.goodreads.com/topic/show/23977993-incomplete-four-invalid-editions

Goodreads Librarians Group – Date Issues: Backmask http: //www.goodreads.com/topic/show/24080358-incomplete-date-issues-backmask

Goodreads Librarians Group – Fix/Add Missing Informations (I Feel You Linger in the Air) http: //www.goodreads.com/topic/show/23294796-open-since-12-07-fix-add-missing-informations-i-feel-you-linger-in-th

Goodreads Librarians Group – Please combine (Romeo and Juliet) http: //www.goodreads.com/topic/show/24115680-done-please-combine

Goodreads Librarians Group – Please Add My Book to My Author Profile http: //www.goodreads.com/topic/show/24366130-please-add-my-book-to-my-author-profile-and-include-the-book-description

Goodreads Librarians Group – Duplicated author http: //www.goodreads.com/topic/show/23739680-open-duplicated-author

Goodreads Librarians Group – Please remove this book http: //www.goodreads.com/topic/show/24304097-please-remove-this-book

Goodreads Librarians Group – new member dealing with http: //www.goodreads.com/topic/show/23988677-new-member-dealing-with

Goodreads Librarians Group – Book linked to wrong author profile http: //www.goodreads.com/topic/show/24347560-book-linked-to-wrong-author-profile

Goodreads Librarians Group – Book linked to wrong author of same name http: //www.goodreads.com/topic/show/24313962-book-linked-to-wrong-author-of-same-name

Goodreads Librarians Group – Unable to claim my novel (incorrect author attribution) http: //www.goodreads.com/topic/show/22964510-done-unable-to-claim-my-novel-due-to-incorrect-author-attribution

Goodreads Librarians Group – Book linked to wrong author of same name (another case) http: //www.goodreads.com/topic/show/24113261-done-book-linked-to-wrong-author-of-same-name

Goodreads Librarians Group – Can't claim my book (same-name collision) http: //www.goodreads.com/topic/show/23273834-done-can-t-claim-my-book-it-is-with-another-author-with-same-name

Goodreads Librarians Group – Someone else has claimed my book http: //www.goodreads.com/topic/show/24320248-someone-else-has-claimed-my-book

Goodreads Librarians Group – Wrong author yet again http: //www.goodreads.com/topic/show/24263604-wrong-author-yet-again

Goodreads Librarians Group – Remove book from author page http: //www.goodreads.com/topic/show/22985269-remove-book-from-author-page

Goodreads Librarians Group – Incorrect author (Arsenal of the Gods) http: //www.goodreads.com/topic/show/23914026-incorrect-author-arsenal-of-the-gods

Goodreads Librarians Group – My novel is attributed to the wrong author http: //www.goodreads.com/topic/show/24087805-my-novel-is-attributed-to-the-wrong-author

Goodreads Librarians Group – Penitence not linked to my author page http: //www.goodreads.com/topic/show/24242441-penitence-not-linked-to-my-author-page

Goodreads Librarians Group – Books assigned to me that aren't mine http: //www.goodreads.com/topic/show/24191849-books-assigned-to-me-that-aren-t-mine

Goodreads Librarians Group – Please separate different books / update ASIN (Iryna Burda) http: //www.goodreads.com/topic/show/24200143-please-separate-different-books-and-update-asin-author-iryna-burda

Goodreads Librarians Group – My books list has disappeared http: //www.goodreads.com/topic/show/24200142-my-books-list-has-disappeared

Goodreads Librarians Group – My book isn't under my profile http: //www.goodreads.com/topic/show/24196879-my-book-isn-t-under-my-profile

Goodreads Librarians Group – Claim a book I wrote http: //www.goodreads.com/topic/show/24113556-claim-a-book-i-wrote